Instinct-Science
and other poems

Instinct-Science

and other poems

by Gurdev S. Boparai

Editor: Neall Calvert
Designer: Jamie Fischer
Cover Photo: "Grasses, Blue Pond, Langley"
by Neall Calvert

First printing 2010

Printed in Canada
ISBN 978-1-894694-78-0

Granville Island Publishing
212—1656 Duranleau
Vancouver, BC, Canada V6H 3S4
Tel: (604) 688-0320 Toll fee: 1-877-688-0320
www.GranvilleIslandPublishing.com

Contents

Preface

I have chosen to write this book in the form of descriptive and loosely interconnected long poems that follow an epic tradition.

I have tried to walk the path of human experience in a continual, interlinked, increasingly intriguing, stepwise continuum from what, in my opinion, is the commonest human trait, i.e., *faith*, to increasingly more intriguing aspects like *logic*, *observation*, *intuition* and *instinct*.

Then I step into the realm of wonderment about the Universe, starting with the most tangible aspect, i.e., *matter*, and proceeding to increasingly complicated concepts like *energy*, *black holes*, *quantum gravity* and what I have named *instinct-science*, in that order. My hope is to build awareness — even by the mention of their names — about the topics thus covered and induce curiosity for further exploration.

— Gurdev S. Boparai

Faith

In one of the folklores of the Punjab
A village existed on the bank of the river Chenab.
A young woman, Sohni, meaning 'beautiful gal',
Was in love with a young man named Mahiwal.
To avoid revelation of their secret romance
And societal rebuke of their stance
Across the river from the village
Mahiwal lived and spent his days.

It used to be pretty Sohni's plight
To quietly sneak out in the darkness of night
And then to cross the river
So she could cuddle in the arms of her lover.
She, of course, had an obstacle to overcome –
Sohni did not know how to swim.
To help with Sohni's regular foray,
A pitcher made of baked clay
Mahiwal did hide in the bushes
On her side of the jungle's lushness
For Sohni to use for crossing the river
So that he could fulfil his longing to be with her.
In dark and dangerous nights thus they met;
Her promises to Mahiwal, Sohni always kept.

When Sohni's swimming ordeal was finished
Mahiwal always for her a fish had cooked.
One day no fish could he catch as usual
But he did not wish to break his ritual.

From his thigh some flesh he did carve
To cook so that she did not starve.
So deep was his dedication to her
Any other way to him did not occur.

As Sohni's ill luck would have it — so sad —
A mean, evil-hearted uncle she had
Who found out the lovers' predicament
And came up with an idea of cruel punishment.
It was known fully well to him
That Sohni did not know how to swim.
In his mind, when drawing the picture,
He also was well aware of the pitcher.
The wily uncle found out the pitcher's location
And invented a scheme to teach them a lesson.

Sadly, it was pretty Sohni's plight
That on a dark stormy night
With the river flowing rough and violent
The uncle sneaked in quiet and silent.
Mahiwal's pitcher he stole that day,
Replacing it with one made of unbaked clay.

From her parents' house Sohni sneaked out.
In the dark stormy night she set out
To swim across the river as usual
To meet her Mahiwal — she wanted to be punctual.
She reached the place where the pitcher should be
In the dark stormy night she could hardly see.
She fumbled in the bushes and found the pitcher
She grabbed it in a rush and dived into the river.
Sohni was naive, her faith she had placed
In Mahiwal's pitcher that had been replaced.

The evil uncle's pitcher of raw clay
Long in the water it could not stay.
It broke right away in the river —
The clay disappeared from around her.
She struggled hard, as she was purposeful,
But all her efforts proved unsuccessful.
In the dark of the night, in the river's sway,
Violent currents swept Sohni away. . . .
For her dedication to be repaid
Valiant efforts had Sohni made.

On the opposite bank, Mahiwal was to wait —
He knew little of his lover's awful fate. . . .
On the tragic night when Mahiwal grieved,
Sohni'd had faith in the pitcher she'd retrieved.
She'd taken a leap of faith because she'd believed
That the pitcher was Mahiwal's — she had wrongly perceived.
She drowned in water storm-beckoned —
Blind faith always needs to be questioned.

Logic

Located in northwest India, in the Punjab,
A typical small sleepy village it was.
Two-storey brick houses were to be seen
One-storey-only mud houses in-between
Of various colours and different sheen;
Some were dirty and some rather clean.
Winding narrow streets with bricks crudely laid;
The middle parts of them open sewers made.
The renovated streets were somewhat wide
But sewers were still running on either side.
Having open drainages a foot or so wide
A drainage system also did the streets provide.
Narrow pathways all dirt-filled
From the streets of the village to the fields they led.
Occasional roads were in patches metalled —
Two-or-three miles distance they often covered
From edge to edges of neighbouring villages;
Most such roads were just patchwork mileages.

In summer season when the monsoons came
The dirt roads were subject to the vagaries of rain.
Whims of the farmers were also there —
Crisscrossing allowed or not, one had to dare.
Sometimes a dirt road would just disappear,
Yielded to crop in a field that was near.
Shortcuts at other times people would take;
Walkways through fields then oft they would make.
In July and August, in the wet season,
Pouring down of heavy rains defied all reason.

People needed landmarks for safe steering
But these would almost be disappearing.
There were big ponds and small puddles —
All of them posed numerous hurdles.

For primary schools in the village to attend
To boys' and girls' schools the parents would send
Their sons and daughters, up to grade five —
Separate education they would provide.
To attend high school after the primary level
To a nearby larger village the children would travel.
To get grade ten education, for instance,
Children often would travel much distance:
To walk two or three miles overall
Was most children's usual protocol.
To the girls' high school all young women went;
All young men to the boys' school were sent.

Often an excuse gave the season of rain
For classes missed and to absent remain.
From doing homework one could refrain —
Travelling in the wet was cause for strain.
An added obstacle was the difficult terrain —
To pile up such excuses the students would train.
For missing classes and homework, if they needed reason,
It was provided them amply by "the rainy season."

There was a student by the name of Jay
Whose attitude was different in many a way.
To other students often his teachers would say,
"Even if Jay has missed school for a day,
Finishing his homework he considers cool —
In spite of having missed attending school.
He visits his classmates in order to find out

What that day's classes have been about."
Because they had a rainy-day, ready-made excuse
His friends, in contrast, would often refuse.

February and March are the months of spring;
Sparse rain and mild weather they always bring.
Blossoms appear on plants everywhere,
Intoxicating aromas waft in the air;
Vast crops emerge in the colour of green
And water flows gently in nearby streams.
Yellow flowers bloom in the gentle heat
On mustard plants close by endless fields of wheat.

Yes, the birds do it and the bees do it,
In the warm spring season they vigorously pursue it.
Then nesting activity in earnest takes over
From mating rituals when they recover.
The life-cycles of birds — this nesting and breeding —
Are timed for a wondrous abundance of feeding.
Lush green shoots of the plants with twigs
Make shelter for hiding birds' chicks and eggs.
A predator's beak cannot easily push
Inside the prickly branches of a thorny bush.
To pollinate the flowers now out in abundance
The bees engage in their endless dance.
In new beehives of theirs, golden honey they collect —
From many different flowers they have gone to select.

The kinds of things Jay found very interesting
Was to visit the places were the birds were nesting
And to run after the peacocks out in the meadows;
When clouds danced above, he'd chase their shadows.
Male peacocks, he knew, did not like to fly —
Chasing to catch them was worth many a try.

If in outrunning a peacock one could prevail
One might just catch it by grabbing its tail.

Tall barnyard grass was abundant often,
It surrounded the fields in every direction.
From vast dry areas of desert sand
It protected the fields of fertile land.
Shelter for partridges it would provide;
They used the tall grass their eggs for to hide.
Their tiny chicks, a fascinating sight,
In earthy brown colours were cute outright.
Catching them was hard no matter how one tried —
They ran very fast and were quick to hide.

In the middle of the fields a mango grove existed
With lemon, guava, orange and other trees interspersed.
To attract birds of many colours and variations
These kinds of trees made fine locations.
Parrots and owls, doves and nightingales,
Cuckoos and those birds with the multihued tails,
And many other birds with names unknown —
To be watching their nests Jay was always prone.
Monitoring birds' nests he considered best
So that he could admire them, and also protect.
Climbing up mango trees was part of the scheme
For close inspection of nests that weren't easily seen.
View of the stream about a mile away
Oft could be enjoyed on a bright sunny day.
Then there were semi-ripe mangoes to suck
If in manoeuvring one had succeeded to pluck.

There was often one buddy or sometimes two
On many such outings who came along too —
Trying to extract honey was adventuresome

From beehives where bees became troublesome.
Bee stings caused swellings all over the face —
And any part of the body that did not escape.
Those stings always required explaining
When facing parents later in the evening.
Sweet honey was occasionally a reward instead
If one ignored in it bees found dead.

The spring season, though filled with celebrations,
Was also the time for final examinations,
Which meant extra hours immersed in one's studies
And less time playing outdoors with one's buddies.
Grade eight examination of the middle standard
Being important, hard work was definitely demanded —
One's name on the honours board in the school corridor
And winning a scholarship required a high score.

While playing and studying was a full-time affair,
The onslaught of puberty also needed care.
For anything or anyone there was no time to spare —
Except for Kim, who was a girl so fair.
Jay had known her since grade four —
To fall for her took just one year more.
When he was in grade five and she in grade six
He began liking her and set out to mingle and mix.
Her attractive features were what drew him in —
Red lips and light-textured, flawless skin.
Her body grew up in timely smooth paces,
Sensual curves formed in all the right places.
Having failed once the grade eight examination
She was prepared now to pass it with determination.

On the day set for the English language test
One of Jay's friends was trying his best.

Some points about English he wanted to discuss
So to get Jay's attention he was making a fuss.
But Jay was trying hard to lock eyes with Kim —
This was the most urgent thing for him.
Amid the mêlée, in front of the examination hall,
Their eyes had met, but no words passed at all.
Because of the societal norms they had to heed
A romance between them was never going to succeed.
Jay also had a reputation of perfection to keep
Expectations of an all-around boy he had to meet.

Because voluptuous good looks Kim now possessed,
Attraction towards her had many young men confessed.
Adolescent village boys would gather and then
The topic of conversation would often be Kim.
Many laid claim to her exclusive attention;
Interactions with her they were happy to mention.
The lion's share of female admirers handsome Jay had,
Who, to vent their feelings, were all too glad.
But his longing for Kim, his secret passion,
He could not express in the usual fashion.
After a soccer game, when boys would gather and sit,
Or at evening gossip sessions around a firepit,
For a decent young man to keep his reputation
He could not be vocal, and showed hesitation.

Women of the water-carrier caste in the village
Usually built firepits for their usage,
For roasting chickpeas or making popcorn
Which people enjoyed to leisurely munch on.
Smouldering embers left in the firepits still
Were used by young men the cold to quell.

Sitting 'round for warmth in the late dark,
In gossip about many things they all took part.
For young men in the village these places were hot —
A pecking order prevailed to assure a good spot.
Many other factors influenced such events
Including various curfews imposed by parents.

Kim passed grade eight but made it just barely;
Her parents were unhappy because she had done so poorly.
The school that she was enrolled in, for instance,
Was in a town about four miles distant.
In placing her there her parents had the intent
Of contact with the village boys to prevent.
To girls in nearby schools Jay did not warm up —
It was obvious to him that they didn't measure up.
For high school examinations, Jay's stakes were raised;
Well-recognized, an all-around boy, he often got praised.
For personal ambition and to meet the raised expectations
He wanted to do well in final examinations.
Many young women often chatted about him
But he wanted to know whether those included Kim.

Communications with Kim were rather sparse —
Both their high schools were now farther apart.
Trying to converse with her he had to struggle;
His daily routine quite often he had to juggle.
To make eye contact when she returned from school
He often made excuses and acted like a fool.
During his cousin sister's wedding
Jay rather carefully was treading.
A chance came by for a room to share
With Kim and her cousins who all were there.
When his mother came by to take him home
The meeting proved to have a dull outcome.

She said he should leave and loiter no more —
Apparently she needed him for an urgent chore.

After the exams there was summer break;
For the results a long time one was required to wait.
To show that such outcomes were correct and proper,
They were carefully printed in a prestigious newspaper.
With the examination verdicts still to come
A guessing game usually it would become.
About a likely date people depended on rumours
Of the timing when scores would reach consumers.
Villagers would rush to the city to buy the newspaper:
Passed or failed? They needed information proper.
It was a big event affecting many thousands;
Quite a buzz was created, much wringing of hands.
Missing a roll number meant one had then failed;
If a roll number was printed then happiness prevailed.
The top fifty students was what it would take
The Merit List from the examinations to make.
Three provinces the university covered;
Merit List students thus felt really honoured.
The newspaper would customarily run
A photograph of the student who was number one.

In his village, with a long-time friend,
Jay proceeded an evening to spend.
Two years older the friend happened to be;
Second-year student in a college was he.
Rumours were strong, people would say,
That examination results were due out the following day.
The friend also revealed during the conversation
That Kim was spending her summer vacation

With relatives in a village somewhere
And he, Jay's friend, had gone to meet her there.
Descriptions of encounters he gave in detail;
Making hints of romance he did not fail.
The way he was putting it — with smiles, for instance —
It sounded like a sure and definite romance.

Topping the Merit List had been Jay's aim,
But a request for a newspaper photo never came.
That gave him the beginnings of a sinking sensation —
He did not stand first as per his expectation.
Details from the friend of his meetings with Kim
Also began constantly torturing him.
All that night Jay did not sleep;
He was heart-broken and continued to weep.

Early in the first year of his college
Jay went home to see his folks in the village.
On the way home from the bus stop
Who should it be but Kim that he'd spot!
Several steps ahead of him she was walking
With her companions, amongst themselves talking.
During the whole of the one-mile route
She had seen him following her group.
Awkward excuses with her group made Kim
So that somehow Jay should catch up with them.
To inform him about her departure to Britain
She wanted somehow to talk to him.
But already he had the information sound:
She was, the following day, overseas-bound.
So all her intentions he knowingly rejected;
Chatting with her he was definitely not interested.

Somehow as they covered that mile
Her efforts to talk to him he made futile.
Youthful romance had lost its magic —
Reflecting upon it, he had not seen the logic.
Rather than an illogical affair to drag along,
Clearly and surely, he had moved on.

Observation

Motorized vehicles like trains,
Cars, ships and also planes
Are integral to modern civilization —
We cannot imagine life without motorization.
The steam engine at its very foundation
Resulted from someone's astute observation:
In a pot was some boiling water;
Steam rose upward as the water got hotter;
It lifted the lid from that pot.
The usefulness of the effect, someone got.
To harness the pressure effect of steam,
Smart people further refined that dream.
Who was the first, the power of steam to tame?
Denis Papin is known to be the scientist's name.

*   *   *

1469 AD — Guru Nanak was born when
He was the first of the Sikh gurus ten.
Of the new Sikh religion, he was the founder,
Contemporary of the Mogul pioneer named Babar.
When a big chunk of India his army swallowed,
Five hundred years of precedence Babar had followed.
Babar invaded India with intention to stay —
Intimidation and carnage were on display.
Guru Nanak saw it to his dismay —
On people's plight he would often pray.
With powerful army and strong administration
Babar was a big force for any confrontation.

Important it was to face up to terror,
Guru Nanak disapproved of Babar's destructive fervor.
A two-pronged approach he had shown,
And Sikh gurus who followed had a similar tone.
Peace-loving holy men who had followers delighted,
Those saints' teachings they carefully highlighted.
The gurus were ridding shortcomings from society
Including rituals and ceremonies of hollow variety.
By removing from society all its rot
They strove to improve people's lot.
By engaging religious leaders in exchanges
Through discussion they wanted to bring changes.

A long-established society as its hallmark
For its roots to sustain and mark
Possesses rational values in its prime
That might become rituals with the passage of time.
Devoid of significance, the rituals lose their meaning;
They might appear hollow to scrutiny and gleaning.
When first started, they might be practical;
With mindless following, they become irrational.

In ancient India there was the myth
Of a bull on its horns supporting Earth.
When one got weary from the weight borne
The bull shifted weight to the other horn.
An earthquake happened at such a moment –
This was supposedly the reason for the event.
For the bull to stand, Guru Nanak argued,
Another surface or Earth it would need.
A second bull would carry on its horn
Weight of that planet that had to be borne.
So on and so forth, thus it would go,
Absurd reasoning for the earthquake, he did argue.

In India of fifteenth and sixteenth centuries
Guru Nanak made such offbeat commentaries.
Myths and beliefs bereft of reason
Guru Nanak shunned as part of religion.
The Guru travelled far and wide,
Two companions often at his side.
Bala was a Hindu and Mardana a Muslim;
Both of them often went with him.
From northwest Punjab where he lived
In all four directions Guru Nanak travelled.
As far as Mecca in the west —
When he reached it he stopped for rest.

Religious leaders of a given village
During his sojourns he would engage.
To enlighten people, he would make comments
In his discussions, talks and arguments,
Against absurdity of rituals and religious strife.
Religion involves God and simplicity of life;
Earning honest living was to be his creed,
And to share one's blessings with others in need;
Thirdly, for a perspective on human fragility
One has to remember God Almighty.
To people of all kinds wherever he could reach
These three things Guru Nanak would preach.

Holy Hindu men of several stripes
Guru Nanak picked for reform swipes.
Ridiculous rituals in which such men engaged —
He challenged them about the way they behaved.
Innocent people they would misguide —
Unsuspecting beings they took for a ride.
Under the pretext of religious bliss
They preached but themselves lived lives amiss.

Simple common-sense and rational thought
Is the approach to life Guru Nanak taught.
To people in Mecca when he was preaching
Omnipresence of God was Guru Nanak's teaching.
For human convenience are earthly directions —
God does not follow man's instructions.

It is said in the Hindu mythology
Gods and demons planned a strategy.
At making holy nectar they did succeed —
After it was done a fight ensued.
One of the gods, quick and swift,
Grabbed the nectar as he left.
A drop of nectar during the haul
Leaked out and to the Earth did fall.
The place on Earth where the nectar did drop —
Triveni is the name of that spot.
Sacred meeting place it is of rivers three:
Ganges, Jamuna and Saraswati.
Travelling to take a dip in the holy rivers,
Hindu worshippers gather every twelve years.
One of the rituals they undertake
Is to take a dip in that place,
At the rising of the sun and facing east
Sprinkling water where the rivers meet.
The belief is that the holy waters
Will reach heaven and one's dead ancestors.

During a trip to the east from his village afar,
He happened to see the Kumbh festival at Hardwar.
Guru Nanak noticed that at sunrise
Facing east, as the custom would guide
Standing in the river during the ritual,
River's water people would sprinkle.

When Guru Nanak happened to ask them
He was given the reason behind the custom —
To dead relatives in heaven people offered
Holy water, that of the three rivers sacred.
Details of the ritual having had heard,
Wading into the river, Guru, facing westward,
Started splashing water while facing west.
People asked the reason for the oddity of the act.
Guru Nanak replied that his fields were drying,
To the west in the Punjab his crops were dying.
People started laughing and began to marvel:
How could the water from the Ganges travel
Hundreds of miles away to fields afar?
Sprinkled water could not reach that far.

Guru Nanak got the chance he was waiting
To back up the observation that he was making.
If water that he sprinkled with an expectation
Could not reach the desired destination
To fields on this planet several miles away,
How could people ask, believe or pray
That sprinkling of water that ritually they did
Would reach up to heaven to relatives dead?

*   *   *

Alexander Fleming, the scientist well-known,
Discovery of penicillin he had first shown.
As a scientist, he was brilliant and bright;
As a lab technician, he was careless quite.
During experiments, it was said,
Forget bacterial cultures he often did.
He worked on these in his laboratory —
The place was in chaos and things in disarray.

Some London artists of name and fame,
Carrying syphilis and living in shame,
Got their treatment from Alexander Fleming —
Profitable side business he was running.

An untested theory of his was also his focus
Antibacterial effects carried by his own nasal mucous.
In 1928, he left on a bench
A bacterial culture plate, a rather non-event.
Staphylococcal bacteria had that plate kept
While on a two-week vacation he had left.
On his return it could be seen
A clear halo was surrounding the yellow-green.
Growth of mould had suddenly begun
Where contamination had been accidentally done.

Now known by the name *Penicillium notatum*
This spore of a rare variant was unknown to him.
A mycology laboratory that had existed
One floor lower, was from where the spore had drifted.
Luck would have it that Fleming had decided
A warm incubator would not be provided.
In no warm place did he store the culture
And London was hit with a cold temperature.
This cluster of coincidences happened in a row;
The mould thereby got a chance to grow.
Rise in the temperature then began;
Staphylococcus bacteria grew like a lawn.
The bacterial growth that took place
It had covered almost the entire plate.
But where mouldy contaminant an area covered,
From bacterial growth the surrounding was spared.

Using deductive reasoning and personal insight
The halo was observed by the scientist bright.
Mould must have released a substance, he concluded,
Growth of the bacteria this substance had precluded.
This observation was to be so great
A change in the course of history it would make.
Active ingredient in that mould which existed
Penicillin was named, as Fleming had suggested.
Infection-fighting substance, extremely potent,
It proved to be a wonderful agent.
Most efficacious infection-fighting drug;
The world responded with a mere shrug.
Discovery of penicillin would alter, as it were,
The fight against bacterial infections, forever.

*   *   *

Across the street to the north of our house
Our neighbourhood park sits about,
One block long in the east-west direction,
Two blocks long in the north-south section.
Up until recently, it had levels two
And quite well demarcated they were too.
The northern part was two feet higher,
Making the southern half that much lower.

Suddenly one fall season it became clear
That many a truck had begun to appear
In the park to deposit lots of soil;
For the next several days workers were to toil.
Mounds of soil in the park were laid
Creating ideal places where children played.
Over several weeks the fun would last,
The children would come and have a blast.

Then fall was over and winter came —
Covered with snow the mounds became.
Over winter months the children could play
As the mounds of soil appeared there to stay.
The bulldozers appeared at long last
And they went to work noisily and fast.
They spread the soil over south half of park
To make it even with the northern part.
When they were finished with the work at hand
Fresh soil was covering half that land.

In early morning hours, to the park,
On feeding trips regularly embark —
Trying to catch an early worm —
Flocks of white birds in a swarm.
After soil had covered the grass green,
Birds stopped coming, it would seem.
Sprouting of wild plants gradually started;
Many a variety was here and there scattered.
Southern half of the park that soil had covered,
Growth of vegetation there suddenly recovered.
With coloured flowers that were quite different,
Wild plants and grasses became very vibrant.

Cultivated grass, although it I adore,
Its monotonous appearance is hard to ignore.
Variety in the scenery suddenly had come —
I liked it and considered it most welcome.
In the midst of the houses it was such a rarity;
The patch of wilderness provided variety.
Lots of birds as well as many an insect,
Plants and their flowers would always attract.
My heart could be felt jumping with joy
As the singing of birds I always enjoy.

Wild plants, flowers and birds to see —
A fascinating summer it was proving to be.
Alas! Then once again out the machines were hauled —
All the wild grasses and plants were mauled.
Regular grass was planted again;
Well-maintained then, the park became.

One of the evenings late that summer —
It would have been around the twilight hour —
About this renovated neighbourly park
I decided to go for a leisurely walk.
As I had finished crossing the street
A handsome young couple I happened to meet.
After polite smiles and brief salutations
We kept walking in opposite directions.

The young woman had appeared extremely sensual —
Blonde hair, blue eyes and a demeanor casual;
Very attractive jaw-line and a sharp thin nose;
Full red lips like the petals of a rose.
Prominent curves and contours of her body
Were too sensual to go unnoticed by anybody.
Firm large breasts were hard to ignore;
One's eyes to her rear end went even more.
Tall blond young man with an easy smile
Had well-developed biceps — he appeared quite virile.

To the southern side of the park I now advanced;
In the dimness of twilight as I glanced
The two young people now lay on the grass
A few metres from the sidewalk, as I passed.
If anybody cared to see and behold
They embraced in a tight and amorous hold.
I started walking briskly there —

It wasn't my business to gawk and stare.
Looking to the south, across the street,
Gazing at the trees there was quite a treat.
In that length of just one block —
Inconspicuous twenty-foot trees, ten in stock,
Held bird's nests in six of them.
In previous years I had noticed none.

Since plants with flowers had grown earlier
There was abundance of food in that year.
When the food chain was set into motion
The birds got busy with procreation.
They also had found an easy neighbourhood
Their eggs were safe and chicks well-fed.
The birds getting a chance to gorge on pests
Would explain the crowding of nests.
In the background I could hear groaning —
Sounds of the young woman ecstatically moaning . . .
Me, I was admiring the capacity of Mother Nature
To adapt quickly so as to readily prosper.

Intuition

Sir Isaac Newton, in 1666,
Age twenty-three, made a trip.
Returning from Cambridge, he went to Lincolnshire
To call on his mother and spend time with her.
One day as he was pensively meandering,
In a contemplative mood in the garden was wandering
Suddenly from a tree, the fall of an apple!
With the notion of gravitation Newton began to grapple —
Why the apple descended particularly
Always to the ground perpendicularly.
Constantly to the Earth's centre the apple is headed —
Upward or sideways path is never treaded.
Defining progress of knowledge and science's march,
That intuitive moment became a significant landmark.
A better example of the power of intuition
One cannot find under any condition.

*   *   *

In 1948, Mahatma Gandhi was shot.
A former French leader expressed his thought.
He had never met Gandhi and did not know his language;
He had never set foot in his country and had no other linkage.
Yet he felt the same sorrow as if, he thought,
Someone near and dear to him had been shot.
On hearing about the death of this extraordinary man,
Mourning all over the world did span.
When Gandhi died as a private citizen,

Without wealth or property he always had been.
He had no scientific achievement or distinction
No academic title or official position.
Yet the thin brown man of seventy-eight
Who walked in a loincloth and had a feeble gait
Was paid homage by heads of all religions;
Heads of state did the same in all the world's regions.
Security Council of the UN, to pay him tribute,
Interrupted its deliberations and gave him salute.
Humanity lowered its flag and people cried;
Mankind was impoverished because a poor man had died.

Gandhi left South Africa in 1915.
Returning to India, he became very keen
On freeing the country from British control —
His efforts and energy he devoted to that role.
His approach to freedom's struggle was unique:
Defiance of the British he directly did not seek.
Prevailing social inadequacies he wanted to reform,
So actions to alleviate misery he would perform.
Distressed millions had problems quite a few;
From their practical problems his policies grew.
For the chores of daily living these people would toil —
To such people's struggles, Gandhi was loyal.
Ideas to help people he did not fret about —
His approach, instead, was to work things out.

The freedom movement in India, rapidly spreading,
By 1930 in several directions was heading.
About violence in the movement, Gandhi was concerned —
That aspect of the struggle, he always shunned.
Progress of the movement, if it ever were to fail,
Violence in the country likely would prevail.
In his home province, called Gujarat,

Sabarmati Ashram Gandhi was living at.
For non-violent struggle Gandhi was prepared,
Motto of the movement he had declared —
India was ready for self-rule, and nothing less.
He had sensed the mood of masses restless.

When poet Tagore, the Nobel laureate,
Who was himself of stature great,
Asked Gandhi about his course of action.
Gandhi expressed his dissatisfaction.
Famously, he was thinking day and night
But did not yet see any ray of light.
With lots of violence in the air,
Darkness surrounded him everywhere.
As an alternative to armed rebellion
He was searching for a suitable pavilion;
For a suitable form of civil disobedience
That would not explode into violence.
For six whole weeks Gandhi searched constantly
While the rest of his countrymen waited impatiently.
The situation appeared quite clear-cut
That India's eyes were on Gandhi's hut.

In an independent India, Gandhi advised
The revenue system would have to be revised.
Its primary concern would be peasants' good —
On this platform had Gandhi stood.
The British system that was present
Crushed the very life out of the peasant.
Even the salt the peasant must use
Its tax rate had become a form of abuse.
The amount of salt upon which the poor would feed
Was much more than the rich man's need.
The money on salt tax that a peasant spent:

Three days' income a year it meant.
The reason that a peasant would use more salt
In comparison to his rich counterpart
Was that under India's scorching tropical sun,
Working in the fields, he perspired often.

Calling it civil disobedience that was non-violent,
Gandhi, on intuition, started a movement.
When a long march Gandhi was to undertake —
March 12, 1930 was the date —
Prayers were sung when the march was to begin;
Mahatma left the ashram with seventy-eight men.
Their particulars and names in the newspaper were published —
Inconvenience for the police was thus abolished.
Two hundred and forty-one miles was the reach.
In twenty-four days to be at the beach
Was the first part of the task they had begun —
Gandhi at the time was sixty-one.
Gandhi and his moving congregation
Followed dirt roads to their destination.
From village to village, as passed these men,
Peasants sprinkled roads and strewed flowers on them.
Two or three times each day
The marchers would make a short stay.
The Mahatma advised the population then:
People were to make and wear homespun.
Alcohol and opium they were to abjure;
Abandon child marriages and live lives pure.

On April 5, 1930 at Dandi
When reached the sea Mahatma Gandhi,
His small band of followers had become a throng —
A non-violent army several thousand strong.

After staying awake throughout the night
And saying his prayers in a manner quiet,
Early in the morning to the sea Gandhi went —
Very little time there, though, he spent.
He dipped into the water and returned to the beach
Some salt he picked up, a small (but big) piece.
Salt that somehow the waves had kicked —
It was from this that Gandhi had picked.
To possess salt not purchased from government
Was a crime that resulted in punishment.
By picking up salt as a token,
The British law Gandhi had broken.
(The craving for salt he already had beaten —
For six years no salt had he eaten.)

Gandhi's intuition had borne fruit —
The two-hundred-and-forty-one-mile route
And the twenty-four days it had taken
Had riveted India's masses' attention.
Trekking across the countryside
He now asked people far and wide
For his signal not to be missed —
This was the handful of salt that he picked.
Publicized defiance of a mighty government —
What a sense of great showmanship it meant.
Dignity and imagination it had required,
But Gandhi was a great artist who was inspired.
Illiterate peasants liked Gandhi's actions;
Also fascinated were the sophisticated factions.
One of his critics was so impressed,
The salt march was comparable, he confessed,
To the return from exile of Napoleon Bonaparte
And towards Paris his subsequent march.

With stealing some salt from a beach
Gandhi's cue was clear but sleek.
Quiet effecitve the message became,
Which clearly was the Mahatma's aim.
India's seacoast and bays masses invaded —
Into the water the peasants waded.
Many a pan and pot they were using
For the salt illegally they were producing.
The police then resorted to arrests and assault,
As Congress Party members sold contraband salt.
Many people were given prison terms
Resulting from such legal concerns.
Some towns also strikes had observed;
Arrest warrants on many leaders were served.
Many legislators left in resentment,
Urging masses to boycott the government.
In some towns arose a situation
Where military and police faced confrontation.
There was violence in some provinces;
Deaths resulted in occasional instances.
Censored were the newspapers that were nationalist;
Sixty thousand political offenders were under arrest.
A month after walking in the sea at Dandi,
The movement started there by Gandhi,
To continue it the people were eager,
Knowing fully well that on mention meagre —
On seeing even a hint of violence —
Gandhi would cancel the movement at once.
Despite beatings, kickings and arrests designed to jolt,
India seethed in angry yet peaceful revolt.
Gandhi's simple intuition was a big reason
Seventeen years later, India got her freedom.

*   *   *

270 to 215 BC were the years
King Hieron II ruled Syracusan affairs.
Of Syracusan noble Hierocles he was the illegitimate son;
Hierocles had a claim to descent from Gelon.
A former general to the Pyrrhus of Epicus,
In the first Punic War, Hieron II was also conspicuous.

In 275 BC it had started —
Pyrrhus from Sicily then had departed.
Syracusan citizens and army groups
All made Hieron II commander of the troops.
He married the daughter of Leptines, the leading citizen,
That helped to further strengthen his position.
Campanian mercenaries had been installed —
The Mamertines they were called.
Under Agathocles those mercenaries were employed —
The stronghold of Messana they seized when deployed.
In harassing the Syracusans they proceeded
But near Mylae by Hieron they were defeated.
If Carthaginians to interfere had not proceeded,
Capturing Messana, Hieron would have succeeded.
But grateful countrymen his success did see,
And they made him king in 270 BC.

Choosing the Mamertines for another attack,
In 264 BC he decided he would come back.
When Mamertines called in the aid of Rome
Punic leader Hanno was befriended by Hieron.
Hanno, with whom Hieron thus had banded,
Recently in Sicily had landed.
By the consul Aprius Claudius Candex being defeated
Eventually to Syracuse Hanno had retreated.
Pressed by the Roman forces in 263 BC
Hieron was compelled to conclude a treaty.
With Rome the pact that he was to sign,

Up to Tauromenium, southeast Sicily was his regime.
Until 215 BC, when Hieron died,
He was loyal to the Romans; he was on their side.
With many provisions and plenty of men,
During the Punic Wars he assisted them.
Defensive purposes of his kingdom to meet,
He kept up a large and powerful fleet.
For construction of the engines to be deployed
His famous kinsman Archimedes he employed.
When seizure of Syracuse by Romans was to start
At a later date, they played an important part.

Given, by a goldsmith, a golden crown,
According to a story, Hieron happened to own.
Without breaking it, Archimedes was told,
To find out if the crown was pure gold.
Into a bath as Archimedes stepped
Rise in water level, he had noticed.
Intuitively Archimedes had understood the cause;
It had dawned on him after a pause,
That if part of his body in water he placed,
It equalled in volume the water displaced.
So eager is he said to have been
To share his intuition so very keen
That he leapt out of the bathtub and naked ran —
In the streets of Syracuse his shouts of "Eureka" began.

Purity of the golden crown he had tested;
Equipment for weighing things already existed.
The intractable problem had been precise calculation —
The volume of irregular objects was a matter of estimation.
Now that volume had been measured by Archimedes,
Density through ratio could be known with ease.
The important problem of an indicator of purity
Archimedes had solved for Hieron with surety.

*   *   *

A few miles away from the Three Gorges Dam
Lived Mr. Ming — a quiet, polite man.
He worked at a small farm, in his mid-fifties;
His wife often helped him in his duties.
Their son, Jao, had a handsome face,
Was bright in his studies and also full of grace.
In his spare time, if he could,
Help his parents he always would.
One day in the fields Mrs. Ming was working
She suddenly felt that her foot was hurting.
A thorn had poked her flesh quite deep,
So that she was in pain and ready to weep.
She pulled out the thorn and went on with work,
But her foot became swollen, continued to hurt.
Over the next several days though she tried many a potion
There was no relief from any such lotion.
Mrs. Ming's discomfort was rapidly increasing;
She also was developing difficulty breathing.
Her transfer to hospital was not very fast,
Her condition got worse and she breathed her last.
Poisoning by tetanus was the cause of her death;
She had never been vaccinated against this threat.

Although Jao was hurting from the loss of his mother,
He continued studying and worked even harder.
He got a job on the water, helping on a boat;
The tourists he catered to, as a host.
From westerners visiting the Three Gorges Dam
Learning the English language was part of his plan.
Money-wise he wanted to be in position —
To go to Canada was his ambition.
In preparation for visiting that country

Saving up money he started in a hurry.
Getting higher education was his aim —
Fruitful his efforts finally became.
A university in Canada accepted his application,
Beautiful city of Vancouver its location.
On arriving in Canada, he was really thrilled,
But to look for a job he also felt compelled,
For expenses of living and to pay for tuition;
He needed to work because of his monetary condition.

A kitchen helper position he was to find,
In a Chinese restaurant — he didn't mind.
The restaurant was owned by a Mr. Wong
Who had moved to Canada from Hong Kong.
Many, many years it had been since
Mr. Wong in Canada first arrived thence.
The restaurant was busy and business was good;
Mr. Wong earned a very decent livelihood.
Mr. Wong's daughter was his only child —
Lydia by name, her nature rather wild.
In school or studies she was not interested,
The restaurant work by her was also neglected.
Doing odd jobs she felt comfortable;
Mostly she liked working at the till.

Early one evening Mr. Wong left the restaurant
To attend a business meeting that was urgent.
The running of the restaurant Lydia was to look after —
About the closing procedure he had advised her.
At closing time Lydia was aware
That, working in the kitchen, Jao was still there.
Jao then went off to use the washroom
Where zipper of his pants got entangled soon.
Skin of his genitalia in the zipper was stuck —

Alone in the washroom, he was out of luck.
Lydia, noticing that Jao she could not hear or see —
Working in the kitchen, he was supposed to be —
Went to the washroom and his dilemma heeded.
Immediately then to help him she proceeded.

When Lydia was bending, Jao's eyes could explore:
Her firm round breasts he could not ignore.
The pinkish nipple forming the peak of each breast —
He could see all through her loose dress.
On cruise boats in China, now and then,
He had experienced older tourist women.
Except for those occasional flings before
He had never seen such spectacle galore.
And Lydia had never a naked man seen —
A virgin until then had she been.
Naked male anatomy in her hands to hold
She could not resist, and did not withhold.
Help herself she did very well,
Until her lips began to swell.
After their clothes both had removed,
To the next step they quickly moved.
She gave a squeak, winced and stood,
Grabbing toilet paper to wipe away blood.

About their romance Mr. Wong was to find,
Although he seemed not much to mind.
Jao, he thought, was a fine young man —
Suitable groom for his daughter's hand.
Soon thereafter they became a couple;
For Jao it proved really beneficial.
Now a resident of Canada, he became eligible —
Even medical school became possible.
Into medical school after Jao got accepted

His father in China he thought should be visited.
To accompany him Lydia did not mind;
Being pregnant, however, she stayed behind.
In China, Jao's father had a new job to manage:
On one of the cruise boats he was handling baggage.
Pictures of his father Jao took with the aim
That his child would see them when opportunity came.
A few months into the medical school
Jao had become a father — rather cool.

Jia, their daughter, they would adore;
When Jao finished medical school, Jia turned four.
To visit in China it seemed about time —
Jia's grandpa she would meet for the very first time. . . .
Mr. Ming had come to the railway station
To greet his family members arrived for vacation.
To his granddaughter this was his first introduction;
Jia expressed vague but interested recognition.
While the family her grandfather was meeting
A keen eye on him Jia was keeping.
Headed to the gate as were all of them
Jia grabbed grandpa's finger and walked with him.
And as warm eye contact between them grew,
That older man was her grandpa, intuitively she knew.

Instinct

Examples there are most conspicuous and distinct
Of miracle outcomes of human instinct.
Theory of general relativity and mass-energy equivalence
Most beautiful and amazing are, for instance.
Deduced by that one greatest among mankind —
The super-human being, Albert Einstein.
Theories his instinct not only produced,
The greatest human being also had them proved
By his amazing mathematical calculations
That leave no room for misconceptions.
His instinctive theories form such a fine sample
There's hardly a need for some other example.

But another illustration that can be given
Shows on a mundane level the message driven.
All over the world millions of times a day
People drive vehicles, as must they.
About driving, as one learns everything,
The training also involves parallel parking.
According to mathematical calculation,
For a precise parallel-parking situation
One has to carefully back in the car;
The length of space that is required for
Such a maneuver — it needs to be
At least one and a half car-lengths, precisely.
In the majority of cases, indeed,
At backing in their cars people succeed.
No one gets out for parallel parking,
Leaving one's car for measure and marking.

Calculating further that the space is sufficient
It is one and a half times that car's length.
The reason for this is quite distinctive:
The whole routine is just instinctive.

*　　*　　*

The instinctive quality we all acknowledge
In non-human species is common knowledge.
The migratory patterns of birds and insects
Clearly indicate some instinctive effects.
As winter begins in the northern climes
Snow geese take flight during such times.
Tens of thousands gather together
And migrate south for warmer weather.
When the season turns they all fly back
To raise their young — but first eggs will hatch.

British Columbia, Canada, a province beautiful
Is endowed with natural scenery plentiful.
In the region called the Lower Mainland
There's Reifel Bird Sanctuary on Westham Island.
A secluded refuge all year round,
Many bird species there abound.
In the month of November it really hums,
Quite a different spectacle it becomes.
A sudden festival of noisy whiteness —
Thousands of snow geese for people to witness.
From north in Russia's Wrangel Island
They're en route south, to Californian land.

Just as there are routes for migratory birds,
Our planet has pathways for animal herds.
And delicate monarch butterflies fly

Through thousands of miles of open sky,
From Canada to Mexico every year —
To them the destination is somehow clear.
Their offspring also instinctively imitate:
A similar route back to Canada they take. . . .
Wild salmon spend the majority of their lives
In the sea, but when the right time arrives,
Swimming upstream many hurdles they meet
Until spawning destination they instinctively reach.

*   *   *

A rather hazy memory of a day in time
Arises: Was it in preschool years of mine?
Going to grandparents' village while talking
With maternal grandmother and mother as I was walking?
A narrow dirt road we were travelling,
The winding and uneven terrain unravelling.
There was abundance of foliage surrounding —
Wild grass and shrubs, and trees abounding.
On one side, our view to prevent,
Ten feet or so tall stood an embankment.
On the other side could be seen
A large crop of wheat, making fields all green.
In keeping with this area's patterns as usual,
In the middle of the fields could be found a well.
Except for irrigating crops from time to time
Wells stayed abandoned most of the time.
Next to a well was attached often,
A reservoir for the water that was open;
As a watering hole which served
For farm animals it was reserved.

In the present-day Punjab region
Wolf sightings, now bygone, were legion.

During those days rumours existed
Because occasional wolf sightings persisted.
Talking while walking, no attention to self,
Suddenly we happened upon a wolf —
It was drinking water at the well
And the three of us into silence fell.
Instinctively we became quiet and scared —
We all knew talking was not to be dared.
Hiding amidst tall shrubs and the grass
Briskly and carefully we picked up our walk.
We kept striding quiet and swift
Till the well way behind us was left.

*   *   *

Through the village from our residence
To our fields was a mile's distance.
While growing up in the village,
At a rather young and tender age,
To go to the fields unaccompanied,
For my sister and I, was a chore indeed.
The dirt road traversed many a sand dune
And in the sand, thorns were strewn.
Abundance of wild plants and bushes to pass
And snakes to fear in the barnyard grass.
Midday in summer in the scorching sun,
Looking around we'd see hardly anyone.
We, the young children, had the instinctive fear
That evil spirits were lurking near.
In the thick shade under a distant tree
With loud shrill laughter they danced carefree.
Stories told about their dishevelled hair,
Tongues hanging out, and big eyes that would stare.
Over their shoulders, their breasts hung backwards;
They were supposed not to say a word.

In addition to our fear of the usual culprits —
Bushes, thorns, snakes and these evil spirits,
There was the fear we'd see an occasional silhouette
Of some evil man during our return visit
During dusk hour with approaching darkness,
Unless some adult would accompany us.
Then, with chirping of birds in the shrubs or a tree
The evening was pleasant and rather carefree.
In the dim coolness we hopped or we walked;
We often made jokes, as we strolled and we talked.

*   *   *

Once several pieces of vacant land
At the periphery of the village did stand.
Using them as an open playground,
The children would cavort there all year round.
By the time my primary school I had finished
Those playgrounds had really diminished.
Most vacant lands people were plowing,
Irrigating them and seeds there sowing.
Areas for hanging 'round in the village
Were undergoing real shrinkage.
But here and there under a banyan tree
Were spots where children could play and run free.
Finally in the evenings the right time came
To engage in a pitched soccer game.
We had to go to a ground designated —
Far from the village it was located.

During one such day after school,
Hanging around casually I played rather cool.
Trio of friends, myself included,
Our quota of homework we had concluded.

As opposed to me, both my friends
Had very closely shaven heads.
One of the friends, with a rather large head,
Wore a turban that was coloured red.
Us three happened to spot a birds' nest,
That a pair of starlings in a tree possessed.
The three of us decided to explore that nest;
Searching for eggs was part of the quest –
Though if any we were to find,
We had no plans for them in mind.
One of the friends climbed up the tree –
Turquoise-green eggs in the nest he could see.
Dropping an egg he did suggest –
The other friend and I were to collect.

For catching the egg, we decided to spread
The red turban from my friend's big head.
At that moment came a rather evil thought;
This idea from my mind I could not block.
Thinking of my plan and the resulting disaster
I simply could not control my laughter.
My big-headed dear friend sensed it,
Caught on to some impending mischief.
As soon as we finished catching the egg,
I rushed to break it on his big head.
He ran away and I missed my aim –
Surely my instinctive laughter was to blame.

*   *   *

A group of my friends in the university
In the Punjab, hailed from a princely city.
They regularly used to go on hunting trips
With wild fowl and deer their favourite picks.

A forested area in the vicinity
Was conveniently located close to the city.
Out of curiosity, but with no hunting interest,
One day I went along with the rest.
We reached the forest in darkness of night —
Occasional game would come in sight.
In the glare of the headlights, a hare would appear
Quickly from the darkness, then disappear.
To occupy our return, no success at hunting,
My friends told a story that was riveting.

The tale involved three friends of theirs
And it happened way back in earlier years.
Those three companions were a rather wild bunch:
They wanted to go on a lion hunt.
During that time in the distant past
For hunting of lions to legally last,
Lion stocks must have been abundant
(It was the second decade of India's independence.)
Several hundred miles' distance was involved
To get their hunting excitement resolved.
A few days' journey was then required
To reach the hunting area desired.
For locating the proper hunting place,
Numerous inquiries they had had to make.

Quite obviously, it would appear,
Their preparations or plans weren't all too clear.
For the lion hunt, a matter delicate,
Their groundwork was rather inadequate.
After the three had prepared the bait,
They perched in a tall tree, upon a lion to wait.
Between the three of them they had brought
Just one rifle there to take the shot.

When a lion nearby happened to roar suddenly
To the ground their rifle dropped accidentally.
Under the tree all night the beast ate and ate —
The lion was helping himself to their bait.
The creature snarled a number of times that night —
So the three of them said when they related their plight.
Repeated roaring of the feline frightened them —
Made them tremble and leak many drops of urine.

Their hunting goal was thus disappointed,
But to stay a little longer was what they wanted.
It was during those few days extra then
They ran into a pair all the way from Sweden.
During the chat they gave the whole account,
The story detailed of their failed lion hunt:
Those drops from each, when the beast was roaring —
Pathetic how overnight was leaking their urine.
Upon hearing about their hunting glitches
The Swedish pair was simply in stitches.
After that bout of healthy laughter,
They proposed to the trio soon thereafter
To travel together on jungle forays —
The five joined up for the next few days.

The Swedish pair was a couple, they were told,
Both had now reached thirty-six years old.
Childhood love into school they had carried;
Right after high school they were married.
He became a banker and she a dentist;
They were visiting India from spiritual interest.

The tourist lodge that they found to stay at,
Adjacent to the jungle conveniently it sat.
The friends shared a room with single beds triple;

In the adjoining space lived the Swedish couple.
One evening after finishing dinner and walking
Sitting in the trio's room, the five were talking.
Sharing their experiences of the day
Engaged in general chat were they.
Then details of the couple's tragic life turn
As the evening wore on the trio was to learn.

The couple's only child they learned,
Earlier in the year seventeen had turned.
University he had been attending,
His first year there was almost ending.
The day when he turned seventeen —
The first day of the week it had been.
However, celebrations for his birthday
Lasted long — right through Saturday.
On the ninth day following his birthday
He was up and ready as on any regular day.
He went to the university as per routine
And returned home early in the afternoon.
When he returned his cousin was with him
And a couple of friends accompanied them.
His mother was working at her practice;
His father was home after a day rather hectic.

With the father of the house still inside,
Quietly the son sneaked outside.
Taking a large soft cushion with him,
He opened the garage door and went in —
Three-thirty then the time must have been.
At six-thirty the mother arrived on the scene.
She opened the garage's automatic door,
Then parked her car as always before.
The engine of the other car she found running;

What else she saw was simply numbing:
Her son there, lying on the floor;
He was dead — their son was no more.
She made frantic efforts, but he didn't revive,
Though she prayed hard that her son would survive.
From his mouth she removed the chewing gum;
She kept it in order to remember her son.
By ambulance to the hospital he was taken
But efforts to revive him had to be forsaken.

Handsome young man he'd been, an all-around winner:
A brilliant student; an accomplished swimmer.
He was studying to become an eye specialist;
That career sat high at the top of his list.
An outgoing fellow, so quite gregarious,
He seemed to be happy, his friends were numerous.
To both of his parents he left no impression
Of someone who was suffering from depression.
Over and over the parents had searches done;
Through his clothing, books and papers they had gone.
They hoped some answers his things would provide,
Clues about why he'd committed suicide.

Though in this age group, depression is known
For his parents the cause was still unknown.
Though they kept agonizing day and night,
The cause of his suicide was nowhere in sight. . . .
It suddenly dawned on the mother one day
That her son had gone out on that Sunday;
His birthday was the Monday that was to follow.
Friends of the son had a memory rather shallow
Of noticing him sad the next couple of days.
From his eyes came a mildly hollow gaze.

Fiddling in his room one day for nothing
The mother happened to notice an unusual something.
On a calendar page pinned on the wall,
In one corner, printed in letters small,
He had jotted down words — quite concisely;
Things he considered important precisely:
Medical school, working out, and the name of a sweetheart
(The one who he felt had broken his heart.)
The mother, then, instinctively suspected
Her son must have felt utterly dejected —
His girlfriend seeing someone else. When he learned,
Sad and heartbroken he had turned.

At the end of this sobering, tragic tale
Quietness in the room did prevail.
Then the woman rose and tapped upon his shoulder
One of the hunting friends, then took him with her
To the couple's room that was just next door.
They went in and then she locked the door.
An hour or so later, back they came;
Everyone in the room still sat the same.
The second friend's arm the woman now grabbed;
To the next-door room he was playfully dragged.
Again they returned after an hour or so;
Some in the room now raised an eyebrow.
Last, there came the third friend's turn.
In an hour's time also, the two would return. . . .
Turn by turn, without any extra fuss,
With all three of them she had had sex thus.
During each man's date, the husband remained cool;
He'd figured out what she was doing — no fool.

Ever since the time of their beloved son's death
They had had no sex life, it was a total mess.

When with all those three men the wife was done,
Foreplay the couple suddenly had begun.
Then they engaged in sex, the trio there present,
Both quite oblivious to the others' presence. . . .
Next morning the couple goodbye bade.
Before leaving, warm hugs to the friends they gave.

Instinctive in nature is sex, it is true.
Is true love instinctive in nature too?

Matter

I got a chance in my final student year —
The end of my studies was finally near —
To set out on a trip to India's south;
In the early seventies this came about.
Southern people consumed less meat than the northern;
Dairy consumption seemed to follow a similar pattern.
Early in the trip, typhoid fever I developed
And I decided that consuming light foods helped —
Consuming dairy products gave safety and pleasure;
It was of the south my first in-person exposure.

As part of their culture, in the area I was visiting,
The dress of some people looked very interesting.
In some upscale eateries, I found it confusing —
Banana leaves for plates they were using!
Initially such customs I found fascinating;
Quickly I got accustomed and found them amazing.
Each time we happened to reach a new place
My friends set out on a search to trace
An adequate supply of milk for me;
For the following days, this would the pattern be.

Finally we made it to the southernmost tip
Where we jumped in the ocean to enjoy a dip.
It was quite the new experience for us
As the area in which we grew up
Was thousands of miles from any ocean —
No wonder we were excited by emotion.
Foolishly I climbed a slippery rock in the sea
Accidentally falling would have been a tragedy.

My typhoid was resolving as we were to visit
The cities and attractions we had on our list.
I had recovered, as healthy as before,
When we reached the famous city of Bangalore,
Modern India's computer technology hub.
To celebrate, my friends took me to a nightclub.
In the bar at a table we were sitting;
Conversation was loud and the noise ear-splitting.

An attractive woman was standing nearby
Who had overheard me as she passed by,
When I happened to say that some milk I needed;
The large-breasted woman appeared to have heeded.
Misinterpreting the comments she had heard
She approached our table shortly afterward.
She looked at me with a mischievous smile.
Without saying a word, she stood there for a while,
Then her heavy, shapely bosom over my face she did sling,
With her long black hair covering everything.
The whole incident passed in just a short while,
But everyone nearby had reason to smile.
For next several weeks they had gossip material.
My friends asked me later how much had been real.
In spite of my illness, the trip was wonderful.
I missed visiting Goa, however, and its beaches beautiful.

Many years later when I decided to vacation
This time around, Goa was my destination.
Attractive sandy beaches and famous warm weather –
A one-of-a-kind experience altogether.
On the same plane on which I did fly
Three young women were in seats close by. . . .
From time to time on television,
Beauty pageants leave no disillusion.

South American women entering such events
Always win their fair share of pageants.
The three women, each had a pleasant demeanour;
Attractive features made smiles even easier.
To beauty contest winners their resemblance was stark,
And soon conversation with me they did start.

About their origin my impression had been correct —
They were from Paraguay was the verdict.
To visit different parts of India they came —
Seeing and learning about the country was their aim.
There was plenty of time during this long flight
About India's people to gain some insight.
Genuine interest was expressed by all three —
Things about India they wanted to learn from me.

Disappointing it was, I must acknowledge,
When I found that of Sikhism, flawed was their knowledge.
Negative notions about the Sikhs they related;
Such aspects they had falsely associated
With beards and turbans that most Sikhs wear.
"I am also a Sikh!" I was quick to declare.
About the Sikh appearance and attributed perceptions,
I tried to clear up their misconceptions.
They were to learn that, largely, Sikh men
Quite well were respected by their countrymen.

Their destination of Goa soon they would reach,
They wanted to spend a few days on the beach.
While staying in Goa our plan was such:
Through e-mail messages we would stay in touch.
The resort I was staying at had settings striking,
With one of the areas especially to my liking.
It was a spot that came totally secluded

Because several fine trees and shrubs were included.
I'd get up very early and finish my workout,
Then at dawn on foot I would set out
Flocks of small birds to see, chirping to hear;
I timed my visits so to Nature I could be near.
This made me as happy as I could have been.
All in all, I had created a serene routine.

Paraguayan friends and I usually went for dinner.
During our time in Goa, we often got together.
In visiting the Punjab they expressed an interest,
And that I accompany them, they did insist.
To go with them now I had to agree,
So a change in my schedule there had to be.
The Punjab's biggest attraction anywhere
Is the Golden Temple, so we planned to go there.

When we finally arrived at Amritsar,
There had just been a nasty downpour.
(Four hundred kilometres from New Delhi situated,
The Golden Temple in Amritsar is located.)
Narrow winding roads had become rather muddy,
Honking noises of vehicles there was steady —
Lanes leading to the most important Sikh shrine
Were all in a frightful state of decline.
In sheer exasperation often I sighed
While my friends remained quietly wide-eyed.

There were throngs of visitors and locals present
Who found the sight of the Golden Temple pleasant;
My friends also found it impressive
And I tried to give a talk informative.
Various aspects of the Sikh faith it involved:
Some of their misunderstanding was thus resolved.

The Sikh attire, rituals and for what they stand
The friends quickly began to understand.
Most effective in clearing away conjectures
Were holy verses quoted from Sikh scriptures.
It proved to be an interesting and blissful visit;
My friends were glad to have the experience of it.

Afterwards, my own or nearby villages to see
I was not really inspired to any degree.
The one I had visited earlier was the exception,
It fitted a "bygone days" description.
Though my relatives here were not so close,
To take my new friends there I chose.
Glimmer of rural life in the Punjab
Still noticeable partially somehow it was.
Not near a city or big route of transportation,
Its location, in relative terms, was in isolation.
The road that connected to the town mid-sized,
At my relatives' village it mostly comprised
Of narrow winding sections of broken concrete —
It seemed to need lots of repair and upkeep.
Trees and shrubs, though, did abound,
And managed both sides of the road to surround.

The house of my relatives we reached at last —
Green fields surrounding it were vast.
Bricks made up the spacious ground floor;
In all, two storeys, with a large entrance door.
A large courtyard, paved with cement,
Had, scattered there, heavy farming equipment.
Narrow stairs climbing one side of the courtyard
To the second level with a deck led upward.
The expansive second floor with its porch open
Was a cosy place for sitting in the evening sun.

With the view from the porch I was quite impressed —
Green fields of wheat for a long way stretched.
And as far as the eye could see, the land was dotted
With many mango trees, randomly plotted.
Various other plants also grew tall there —
Small patches of them popped up everywhere.

Our hosts were happy when it came to greeting us;
We were made to feel comfortable without a lot of fuss.
Feeling their warmth, my friends were impressed
With their hospitality, their generosity stressed.
Provisions for us were far from stringent:
Chivas Regal whiskey at our disposal was abundant;
Fresh food was simple, with menu typically local —
In singing its praises my friends became vocal.
In sumptuous quantities the meals were devoured;
My friends' threshold of formality was lowered.
Largely meals were a vegetarian affair,
Although many times our good hosts there
Made special efforts to bring chicken and goat meat,
Then cooked it superbly for us to eat.
Eggs being present at the breakfast table;
Often they were quite readily available.
Contented and comfortable became all four of us;
My friends found my Jat relatives marvellous.

On long walks in the fields we frequently went,
On the banks of a canal some time was spent.
This nearby channel had water flowing steady,
Though the slow-flowing water was slightly muddy.
The temptation my friends could no longer stall
They must have a rowdy swim in the canal.
One day when the bright sun really glared
At midday my friends set out prepared.

Wearing bathing suits, they were really pumped;
Into the waterway the three of them jumped.

I also came prepared that day for a swim,
But stayed on the bank and did not join in.
They enjoyed themselves in the water one and all
As I stood on the banks of the broad canal.
Then one friend approached with a grin on her face
And grasped me tightly in a warm embrace.
Like the other two women, she was pretty hot stuff.
This tall, shapely goddess tried to lift me up!
I asked her casually, "What is the matter?"
Laughing, she replied with audacious chatter,
Telling me that *I* was the matter for her.
When I asked for elaboration on her answer,
She replied giddily that I have weight,
And I was taking up space in her embrace.
Saying that, she dragged me into the canal
And soon playing in the water were one and all.
The lukewarm water and the day's bright sun
Produced sensual sensations in everyone.
The four of us engaged in lots of foolish stuff
And remained in the canal till we'd had enough.
To a nearby well we headed soon thereafter
To thoroughly wash ourselves with its clean water.
We'd had the foresight to bring as precaution
Chivas Regal, which helped relieve any exhaustion.

*   *   *

My friend's description in terms scientific
Was a definition of matter quite specific:
Matter is the entity the description implies —
It has mass, and space is what it occupies;

Of matter is composed every physical object;
Matter is loosely defined for purposes specific.
About its description, one can converse —
Matter constitutes much of the observable universe.
When there is, however, need for precision
The term *matter* physicists do not use for definition.
In more clearly defined terms they speak —
Mass, energy and particles are the concepts they seek.

Four of the five different *states* are known better —
Solid, gas, liquid and plasma — as matter.
The four forms are recognized quite readily,
The fifth is more complicated scientifically.
Description of matter by physicists has included
All that is of elementary *fermions* constituted.
There are *leptons*, including electrons,
And some forms of *quarks* make protons and neutrons.
Protons, neutrons and electrons when combined,
The formation of atoms and molecules is destined.

In matter there are other entities included —
Controversy-laden sometimes this has concluded.
Without being matter some entities may have mass —
This concept also often comes to pass.
From combination of quarks is formed a *hadron*.
Because of a certain scientific phenomenon,
Quarks unbound from other quarks never exist.
The proton and the neutron are on the hadron list.
Usually these nuclei are surrounded,
By clouds of electrons to them bounded.
A nucleus that has as many electrons
As there is presence of number of protons
Is electrically neutral and called an atom;
Otherwise the name *ion* is given to them.

Leptons, from other particles, can exist unbound.
On Earth, electrons in atoms are mostly bound,
But generally it is not difficult to free them —
Easy is the task to obtain that freedom.
This fact is exploited in the cathode-ray tube.
Briefly formed states of *muons* may include
Muonic atoms, called thus when they are found.
Neutrinos to other particles are never bound.

Properties which homogenous matter constitute,
To any amount of such matter sticks every attribute.
For example, as brass it may be a mixture
Or it could be elemental like iron pure.
Heterogeneous matter, however, such as granite
It does not have composition that is definite.
Matter, in bulk, can be present
In several phases that are different.
Such different phases can change according to pressure
Or they depend on the degree of temperature.
A phase of relatively uniform composition chemical
Has an existence that is macroscopically physical
And uniform physical properties, included in which
Are *density*, *crystal structure* and *refractive index*.

Three familiar names are included in these phases —
Solid, liquid and gas are these stages,
Detailed variations that are scientifically
Included in such phases automatically.
As conditions alter, matter may change —
From one phase to another may be that exchange.
In small quantities, matter may exhibit
Properties that entirely differently exist
From those in the bulk material state
And may or may not be described by any phase.

In scientific terms, which are confusion prone,
Phases sometimes as *states of matter* are known.
Chemical matter is the part of the Universe
That, as we know, is made of atoms diverse —
Dark matter and *dark energy* not included.
Black holes are similarly excluded,
As is *degenerate matter* in many a form —
Dwarf and *neutron stars* to this category conform.

Total mass of the Universe so far observable,
According to studies, this is calculable:
Chemical matter forms four percent;
Calculation of the remaining content
Shows that dark matter is twenty-two percent
And seventy-four as dark energy is present.
Then there is *anti-matter*, complicated scientifically,
Which is not found on Earth naturally —
Except very briefly, if at all,
In quantities that are vanishingly small.
This is because anti-matter which came to exist
On Earth, outside a suitable laboratory's midst
Would vanish almost instantly
If it was to meet the Earth's matter ordinary.
In tiny amounts some anti-matter is stable,
And *anti-particles*, in amounts comparable,
Can be made, but not in large quantity;
It can only help test many a property.

In science, there is considerable speculation —
It is also there in science fiction:
Why is the observable Universe almost entirely matter?
And if there are places that are mostly anti-matter,
What are the possibilities that there exist?
And is anti-matter something that scientists can harness?

In the Universe, the apparent asymmetry
Between matter and anti-matter remains unsolved mystery.
Of incredible amounts of dark matter's existence
There are many indications in science.
From the early Universe, there is evidence to pass
This matter probably has energy and mass.
But different is the composition of the dark matter
Than the smallest particles that form ordinary matter.

In spite of the scientific knowledge to dissuade,
Of matter only some folks think our world to be made.
Animal and plant life and energy are there —
Of all those most human beings are aware.
Anytime people think about life around them
Only matter do they visualize then.
Involved in a baby's fumbling first step
There is energy, but it is the cuteness —
Shape and form to visually measure —
Of that baby that gives us pleasure.

Energy in various forms to us brings
Pictures on television showing people and things,
But it is the image of matter in them
That fires up people's imagination.
Between matter and energy complicated interactions
Are always involved, in productions
Such as blooming flowers beautiful and fragrant.
Fascination they provide, invoking amazement.
Just as there is matter in particles of fragrance,
It is also present in the aesthetic appearance.
The flowers that give us a thrill,
Matter in them we visualize still. . . .

Mechanical energy might cause a bone's fracture;
The sufferer would remember the offending structure.
Most other concepts are like a ghost;
To ordinary people, *matter* matters most.

Energy

Of life and the nature of the Universe,
Along with matter, energy is the obvious aspect.
In the case of green plants, the radiation the sun supplies
Is an external source of energy on which a creature relies.
Some form of chemical energy for consumption
By animals is needed for growth and reproduction.
The daily calorie requirements by humans are taken
Through food products combining with oxygen.
Intake of fat products a convenient example makes,
Another such example is carbohydrates.
Such food molecules in the body are *oxidized*;
They end up producing water and carbon dioxide.
Some of the energy in the body is indeed
For chemical reactions, it serves the deed.
The rest of chemical energy is converted into heat
From sugars and fats that living beings eat.

About living organisms, it is quite evident
In the use of energy they are remarkably inefficient.
About chemical energy is true this proclamation
It also applies to energy of radiation.
More efficient than living beings are machines' mechanisms.
In the case, however, of growing organisms
The energy that is finally converted into heat
Has a vital purpose: It has to complete.
With regards to the molecules they are built from,
Highly ordered, the energy allows tissues to be grown.

To concentrate in one specific place,
For matter and energy it would necessitate
Greater amounts of energy as heat to disperse
Throughout the remainder of the Universe;
More evenly spread out as the outcome
Across the Universe is their pattern.
This is one of the laws of Nature,
It pertains to both energy and matter.
Energy differences attained by simple organisms
Can be better than those by the complex ones.
The cluster of events in a metabolic pathway that began
Is the physical reason behind the food chain —
A portion of chemical energy turning into heat
Such conversion happens at stage each.

Energy is the ability to do work as needed —
Several different forms of energy are included:
Gravitational, potential, thermal and kinetic,
Nuclear, chemical, electromagnetic and also elastic.
Groups and forms of energy the names contain;
Natural phenomena all their forms explain.
Various, these forms of energy together
Are convertible from one form to another.
Strong electric fields cause breakdown of air,
Production of plasma takes place there.
When formation of plasma has thus occurred,
Energy from the electric field to heat is transferred.
Caused by the heat and light's production,
Air molecules' random type of motion
Becomes the cause of mechanical energy's production —
The specific combination is thus lightning in action.

A famous scientist is rather loosely quoted here
About the concept of energy, a fact that is clear:

About natural phenomena that are known to date,
A governing law exists, make no mistake.
To this law there is no known exception —
It is exact so far, to our perception.
It is called the *law of conservation of energy* —
According to it, something all around happens to be.
That something is called *energy* by name,
The quantity of which does not ever change.
Through Nature's changes, manifold and mixed,
Energy's quantity always remains fixed.
Most absurd idea is the above spectacle,
Which exists due to a mathematical principle.
It is about a calculation strange:
When something happens, things do not change.
It is not a description of anything concrete
Nor of any mechanism discrete.
It just is a strange fact to wonder
That when we calculate and arrive at a number,
After watching as Nature goes through her tricks —
When we thus have had our kicks —
Then we calculate the figure again —
Lo and behold! That number is the same.
Energy is conserved because laws of physics,
Between different moments of time do not distinguish.

The concept of energy — its transformations as well —
In explaining and predicting are extremely useful.
Most of the natural phenomena that come by,
Energy and transformations can easily imply.
A given kind of energy, when transformed
Into whatever kind it does, we are informed;
Often guided by entropy's considerations
Are energy's directions relating to such transformations.

There are well-defined laws of physics,
Energy equally spreads in their context.
Large-energy transformations are doomed to fail;
Things only happen on a proportionally smaller scale.
Random movement of energy or matter, statistically,
In concentrated forms or smaller space, is unlikely.
This concept of energy has a big influence,
It is used in all the fields of science.
In chemistry, the energy differences
Determine the forms of various substances,
Whether and to what extent they can react,
Or into which other substances they can convert.
During metabolic processes in biology,
Changes in available energy to study,
Broken and made bonds chemical
Are used to conduct studies analytical.
In the form of various molecules,
Energy is often stored in our body's cells:
Sugars and fat molecules give up energy and hydrogen
When they appropriately react with oxygen.

Earthquakes, volcanoes and mountain ranges
Are included in continental-drift-related changes.
Phenomena in geology and related fields
Information for these studies yields.
Incidences can be explained in terms quite clear
Describing energy transformations in Earth's interior.
Natural phenomena like blowing wind, heat and rains,
Snow, lightning, tornadoes and hurricanes —
Are brought about by solar energy on Earth,
From energy transformations they all result.

Supernovae, quasars and gamma ray bursts —
The phenomenon of stars throughout the Universe —

Are energy transformations of matter taking place:
Large-scale occurrences, in outer space. . . .
These transformations of various kinds are the reason
By which phenomena like solar energy are driven.
In various classes of astronomical objects
Gravitational collapse of matter also results.
Examples of this are diverse star formations
Or black holes — sources of energy in such transformations.

The other form of energy conversion is nuclear fusion,
Which happens in lighter elements, primarily hydrogen.
Energy transformations in the Universe, over time,
Are characterized by *potential energy* of many a kind.
The origin of the Universe happened whence —
The above phenomenon is available thence.
Potential energy gets released when a suitable
Triggering mechanism for it becomes available.
When released, the energy gets transferred
Into more active types, whichever is preferred.

Aside from happening in the outer Universe,
In a slow process, in the core of the Earth,
Heat from nuclear decay in some heavy elements
When released, may lift mountains in moments.
This lifting represents potential heat energy
That was released into active form when ready.
Cause for an earthquake also energy provides —
A triggering event occurs, followed by landslides.
The stored form of energy is released in rocks;
They come from the same radioactive stocks.
Such events represent energy stored in heavy atoms —
The collapse of stars first created these items.
The other energy source, from the beginning of the Universe,
Via the Sun its forms reach the Earth,

Created from the nuclear fusion of hydrogen —
Sunlight is the result of that fusion.

Energy, again, may be stored after reaching Earth.
Water, for example, evaporates from the ocean first;
This is followed, as we know, by clouds' condensation,
Then deposited on mountains, resulting in formation
Of rivers and streams, which in dams are used
To turn turbines and hydroelectricity is produced. . . .
Certain weather phenomena are driven by sunlight,
Including the events demonstrating a hurricane's might.
When large warm areas of oceans unstable
Heated over months, give up energy thermal,
This powers a few days of violent air flight —
Cyclonic storms are unleashed, causing much fright.

Plants, as we know, over time capture sunlight
Which can be released as heat and light
In a forest fire when triggered suddenly. . . .
Converted and stored energy living organisms use regularly.
Energy changing from one to another version
Brings up examples of mutual conversion.
Mechanical energy can be converted into the same type
By a lever placed at a different site.
Mechanical energy from the application of brakes —
Conversion into heat energy it makes.
Chemical energy is what is stored in matches;
Sunlight changes into nuclear energy by the use of gadgets;
Conversion of heat energy can take place
Into chemical energy with a blast furnace,
Mechanical energy via steam machines,
Electrical and nuclear energy produce through various means.
Several examples can be given of mutual conversion to show
Electrical, electromagnetic and nuclear energy produced also.

Putting all scientific considerations aside
Energy is an integral part of daily life.

*　　*　　*

Related to the topic of energy, by chance
I once came across this shocking incidence.
Many times I used to joke with my patient Chris
That I was the first person he had ever met.
When he first came into this world
My two hands did the newborn hold.
His mother, a pleasant blonde woman,
For childbirth she did careful planning.
During labour, there was some delay
Orders to come out the baby couldn't obey.
A call for a specialist's help was relayed
But the specialist, somehow, got really delayed.
Using instruments, and some luck, maybe,
I ended up delivering the baby.
All in all, things went very well;
The experience was, for all concerned, swell.

Like almost all other growing tots
There were, for Chris, the usual childhood shots.
Teasingly I reminded him during his growing years,
That he got his shots through his cries and tears.
Quite normal growth, his health history relates;
There were the usual cuts and scrapes.
Occasionally he got needles in the butt
Or pokes for anaesthetising, to suture a cut.
Sometimes there were crying sessions
And treatments resulted in protestations —
Snot running down from Chris's nose;
Copious tears from his eyes flowed.

When he was done with many such procedures
His mother would clean his face afterwards.
The visit always ended on friendly terms —
Between Chris and I, no remaining concerns.
I often felt for the child's generosity
And I also had tons of sympathy.

A wholesome young man, pleasant and fine,
Chris kept growing with the passage of time.
Blond hair reflected genetic inheritance
General good looks also came from both his parents.
He liked to play sports and, because of generous height,
He was basketball team's star shining bright.
Athletically built, he also played other sports;
For physical activities he was an all-rounder of sorts.
Matching his facial features and blue eyes unique,
He had developed an attractive physique.

At age seventeen, he got a girlfriend,
Falling in love in age-appropriate trend.
Although we had always communicated openly,
To probe his love life did not seem appropriate to me.
Even though I had never seen her,
Nor I had looked at any of her pictures,
My guess was that Chris's girlfriend
Was very attractive and the popular kind.
Chris did not have any inhibitions
That he showed during our light-hearted discussions.
In fact, there was a bond between us:
Simple, mutual warmth expressed without too much fuss.
About his health whenever I asked,
He felt very comfortable and relaxed.

His drawings from school he usually brought
To show me all the stars that he got.
In his earlier years, greeting cards
He brought on special occasions, to give his regards.
In later years he would sometimes relate
Interesting things that had taken place.
Things that happened when he played sports,
Since he took part in activities of all sorts.

He, however, was only a mediocre student —
In grade twelve science he lacked confidence.
It must have been a month or two
Before his final examination was due,
That he came one afternoon to my clinic
Walking in casually, showing no panic.
I was in my usual relaxed mood,
Glad to see him looking healthy and good.
He appeared to have come straight from school,
Which felt to me a bit unusual.
In the examination room I did not see
The usual relaxed self I expected him to be.
That cheerful confidence and warm expression
He lacked that day, was my impression.
That gave me real cause for concern —
A delicate approach I took, in turn.

The first suspicion that came to my mind:
He might have had a tiff with his girlfriend.
I tried to broach the topic carefully,
And right away he hinted to me
His girlfriend and he were doing great —
Things more complicated did the problem make.
Straight from school he had come,
Rather to the doctor than going home.
If that had been his first priority,

Medical issues were my first curiosity.
That there was no obvious physical discomfort
Was my clinical impression prompt.
Because he did not appear depressed,
Might be sexual performance he wanted discussed.
Sometimes during such delicate occasions
I ended up making special provisions,
Leading the patients and making them
Comfortable enough so they can discuss the problem.
That was not the case either —
Sexual performance was not the cause for bother.
On the contrary, he felt comfortable enough.
It was something from earlier that day he came to discuss.

His science teacher was a young female,
Attractive fantasy of many a young male.
On Chris's good looks she often commented
And his sex appeal she also complimented.
Chris had not minded her mischievous glances
And the lewd smiles she gave in many instances —
These served to massage his raw young ego.
A few times earlier, not long ago,
She had reminded him, in language stern,
In the subject of science he had lots to learn.
The topic of energy in the class
Was being covered when this came to pass.
Early during that day she suggested to Chris,
It was better that after school they meet —
She had wanted to discuss something with him.
It was likely, Chris thought on a whim,
She probably wanted to chide him and remind
How badly in science he was behind.

The teacher took Chris, as arranged before,
To a vacant room and locked the door.
Facing each other while they were discussing,
She sat wide-legged, their knees were touching.
The teacher was wearing a nice pantsuit,
It suited her shapely figure and her face cute.
Either forgotten or her decision not to wear —
Her immaculate attire was devoid of underwear.
The zipper of her pants was open wide
And she had made no effort to hide
What was revealed through the open zipper —
Not for a moment did it appear to bother her.

Chris felt nervous and quite awkward;
He could not pay attention or say a word.
The teacher appeared quite calm and casual
Chris was simply dazed by the visual.
The teacher had advised (from what he could remember)
Steps in learning science he was to ponder.
While he was consumed by the visual graphic
She appeared to be talking about a given topic.
In the class, that subject was being covered.
Her demeanour was rather strange, he discovered.

On the topic of energy, covered in various fashions,
She told Chris about private lessons.
By dimming all the lights from bright
She had suggested they cover electricity and light.
The chapter on sound could be okayed
While in the background music played.
And when and as things did progress,
Mechanical energy and heat they would discuss.

Chris had managed to keep his composure
He somehow succeeded and did not allow her
To read the state of his mind during the talk.
When the session was over, he decided to walk.
Proving a mark of mutual warmth and his trust,
He came to see and discuss with me first.
I did not at all let Chris notice
The strangeness I felt, affecting my thoughts.
Spending enough time with him I felt
Was needed for him to properly gather himself.
After appropriate discussion with Chris,
I contacted his parents to handle all this.
The delicate matter had left its effect —
The young man deserved affection and respect.

Sexual attraction can be strange
And make people's sense of propriety change.

Black Holes

Pleasant, easy-going and a young man fine,
Tony was a long-time patient of mine.
He dropped in to see me occasionally
For minor illnesses that often come seasonally.
Huge chest muscles and big biceps flexing
Were evidence of regular weightlifting.
In exercise since a very young age,
I am in the habit to regularly engage.
But in developing huge muscles I have no interest,
Especially the ones I have on my chest.
Since Tony's health problems were usually
Easy and minor, they were treated easily.

Chatting one day, as we did quite often,
He showed me the picture of a woman.
She was young and appeared very pretty —
Perfect chiselled features, green-eyed beauty.
He told me that she was a medical student
Who lived in another country, on a different continent.
I thought Tony was going to marry her
And was disappointed to learn later
That Tony's marriage never materialized.
It did not happen with the Russian green-eyed.

Tony was a member at a popular gym —
Telling me the stories, he drooled often
About all the beautiful women he encountered —
He seemed ecstatic as we conferred.
From our conversations, quite probably,

He knew that I exercised regularly.
Once he offered to take me to that gym
Enabling me thus to see it from within.
To give me a short-term trial free
He brought several days' passes for me.

I had plans to go to Hawaii,
In a few weeks I was scheduled to fly.
That gave me an incentive unique
To try to shape up my physique.
Starting several days before leaving for Hawaii
I went to the gym daily, for a try.
The place was amazing and vibrant —
From looking around this was quite apparent.
The place was packed with young healthy women
And, of course, there were equally healthy men.
There was stimulating music playing
Where aerobic exercises a large group was doing.
They were in one part of the gym
And in another part, quite close to them,
Were people riding stationary equipment,
While close by, in another segment,
A variety of weights and gadgets were set —
These were helping many people sweat.
Shower, sauna and a pool in which to swim
Were located in a separate section of the gym.

The gym's atmosphere was a high-energy hub;
A meat market it was, similar to a nightclub.
Depending on an individual's preference
There was, however, a remarkable difference.
Dressing up for a nightclub, people who are keen
Will wine and dine, to see and to be seen.
In the gym, people were dressed to perspire;

That, however, was not the only thing to inspire.
They were also there to see and be seen —
The view was akin to a movie close-up scene.
There were no drunken hassles with which to bother
Because people at the gym were sober.
To my mind, it was an excellent place;
In deciding, I had no ambiguity to face.
I had liked the place so much,
Soon I acquired a regular membership.

Part of an educational conference
My trip to Hawaii was in essence.
I knew several of the attendees there;
It was a very congenial affair.
The brief air turbulence during the flight
Had caused among passengers a little fright.
The trick for some is to use a couple of drinks —
That might let you have your forty winks.
A trip to Hawaii is memorable for anyone —
The climate is perfect with its warm sun.
The colour of the water is turquoise-blue,
And the snorkelling experience brings to view
A wonderful variety of colours bright —
Many kinds of fish are there in sight.
In the water and on the beaches around
Plentiful beautiful bodies abound.

One evening a luau was the setting to meet
At a perfect location on the beach.
Pleasant and mildly cool the air was getting
The sun over the ocean was just about setting
Ocean waves were making a constant sound,
Nature playing a symphony in the background.
At the stage, there were several performances,

Including many smooth rhythmic dances.
Making sort of a semi-circle around,
We all took seats upon the ground.
In our group, also drinking and eating,
Were several of my senior colleagues from the meeting.

Everyone was having a jolly good time.
There was a pretty hula dancer in her prime —
She appeared to be the most attractive in the group.
Making eye contact, she gave me a look.
Approaching me she burst with laughter
And took me to the stage to dance with her.
Finding it very hard my balance to keep,
Being tipsy, I was unsteady on my feet.
A couple of times when I was to flip
She kept holding me tight at the hip.
That grip on me for a long time she kept —
People there joked it was simulated sex.
Her grip during the episode she would enhance
Finally we finished the smooth, rhythmic dance.

On the Hawaiian beaches spending my holidays,
Relaxing I was for several more days.
One day I happened to notice a pretty woman
Walking on the beach, she had tresses woven.
She was one of those pretty young things
Endowed with lovely prominent rear ends.
Hers appeared to be in beautiful harmony
With the rest of her attractive anatomy.
She had long legs and sturdy thighs;
Her narrow waist and big breasts were attractive to guys.
She also had perfect facial structure —
Even white teeth Nature had given her.
She just glanced at me and kept walking.

On a cell phone she appeared to be talking.
I suddenly realized that I had seen her
Coming to the gym, where she was a regular.

Returning from Hawaii after days ten
I continued my workouts at the gym.
One day after a workout quite taxing
I went to the hot tub area for relaxing.
The woman I had seen in Hawaii
Was sitting in the hot tub, nearby.
I said hello to her and we started talking —
I told her that I had seen her walking
On a Hawaiian beach a few days earlier.
She said she also had seen me there.
It came out during our conversation
That she was in Hawaii, also on vacation.
A close friend was with her during that time;
That friend happened to be a patient of mine.

The woman talked about not feeling well
A sore throat that day was making her unwell.
I politely offered to see her if in need —
To my surprise she readily agreed.
As we had discussed, the following day she came.
She kept her appointment — Lisa was her name.
As I have mentioned, Lisa's friend
Was a patient of mine and used to bring
Many of her relatives and friends to me —
A sizable group of patients it happened to be.
They all were people with Ethiopian background.
Overly confident I do not wish to sound,
But noticing the body contours of the young women,
I had observed a remarkable phenomenon.
On breasts and buttocks, they carried ample flesh
Not much fat their narrow waists did possess.

My schedule was busy on the day of her appointment —
A packed agenda to me was quite apparent.
Lisa's appointment was early in the morning
And she showed up with meticulous grooming.
A combination of good genetics and regular exercise
Her neat and modest clothing could not hide.
In order to do a check-up proper,
In the examining room, as I had asked her,
She sat comfortably on the examination table.
Grabbing a tongue depressor and a light suitable
A good view of her throat in order to provide,
I asked her to open her mouth quite wide.
Looking at her throat as she opened her mouth,
"It is a red hole," I blurted out.
Momentarily she appeared taken aback.
Soon she seemed to have understood that
I meant to say her throat was infected —
That's what the deep red colour had reflected.
She quipped back, as she was laughing,
That about red holes she definitely knew nothing.
However, as far as black holes are concerned,
Enough knowledge about them she had earned.

It was my turn to be mildly surprised —
She was studying physics, I was apprised.
While we were talking, she further related
From Ethiopia, as a child, she had immigrated —
She had come with her family when she was nine.
Always a bright student and athlete fine,
While at school, in sports she excelled.
During her university years, she was compelled
To work out at the gym in limited fashion
But studying black holes was her main passion.

I took a swab from her throat
To get it tested for bacterial growth,
And promised to call her when results came back —
The following day I made the contact.
I phoned Lisa to inform her about
The arrival of the test results from her throat.
During our talk I showed curiosity
About the black holes on which she was an authority.
I knew nothing about black holes —
In this we were at opposite poles.
Out of the blue she made an offer to teach;
Soon thereafter, we decided to meet.
During several days, as things progressed,
She taught me about black holes, as promised.

Albert Einstein's general theory of relativity
Made the prediction that the gravity
Of an extremely dense body could bend a ray of light —
Do it severely, leaving no escape in sight.
Black holes are named the bodies so dense
That extremely indirect in the Universe is the evidence.
Astronomers can never see them because
Light does not escape them, the underlying cause.

Take something like the sun, for instance —
It could collapse if it shrank
Into a ball of the approximate size,
Measure it would, one and a half miles wide.
For our Earth to become a black hole
Its new mass, on the whole,
A sphere of such size it would be
No bigger than a pea — yes, a pea!

Scientists have calculated that such a drastic compression
To the biggest stars only could happen,
Once hydrogen and other fuel ran out.
They have posited that once the stars sputtered out
The remaining gas would collapse under its own gravity
To the infinitely dense point we call a *singularity.*
Telescopic observations in such cases, clearly
Useful they are to back up the theory.
Discovery of quasars, the beacons extremely bright,
Billions of years' distance they have, at the speed of light.
The possible source, scientists have suggested to us,
That provides power for something so luminous
Is a concentration of millions of suns as a whole,
All pulled together by a super-massive black hole.

Some stars seemed, the scientists found,
To have invisible companions they whip around.
They concluded that, in our Milky Way,
Only under the pull of gravity could they
Keep in such tight orbits
From a black hole that pulling begets.
To add to the black holes' evidence
Sometimes the scientists resort to measurement.
At up to a 1.1-million-miles-per-hour rate
The innermost parts of galaxies rotate.
The startling speeds of the cores point to a sum
Up to a billion times the mass of the sun.
The super-massive black holes, as a scientist sees,
Form the core of almost all galaxies.
The lightest black hole so far discovered,
Scientists have its dimensions measured.
Compared to our sun, its mass is about four times greater,
While measuring about 15 miles in diameter.

Since Albert Einstein's equations black holes have shown,
It has become a fact well known
That black holes slow time, and still it stands
That they stretch large objects into spaghetti-like strands.
Losing mass and shrinking since their prime,
Black holes are expected to evaporate over time.
The nearest galaxy to ours that has been located –
Ten million light years away it is situated.
The black hole at its centre, the son of a gun,
It is 60 million times the mass of our sun.

Black holes are formed when very large stars die.
There are some steps and stages whereby
The star first collapses and then outer layers rebound
To form a supernova explosion, to be found
Left at the core, process thus begun,
It would form a black hole, or else a neutron.
On measurement of the critical mass of the star
One or the other would depend by far.
To form a black hole, the mass left at the core
After the explosion must be more
Than three times the sun's quantity.
Most of its life, it needs to be
Fifty to one hundred times the mass of our sun
Eventually for it to a black hole become.
It is impossible that a black hole will
Form from Earth within years several.
And in the neighbourhood, possessing the right stuff,
There are no stars large enough.
Some of the brightest stars in the sky –
They might become black holes, by and by.
For a couple of stars in the constellation Orion,
It might not happen for millions of years of trying.

Black holes can be of various characteristics
And can be divided into several size statistics.
Super-massive black holes, as mentioned before,
Contain hundreds of thousands of stars or more.
Billions of times the mass of our sun are they,
Present at the centres of galaxies, including our Milky Way.
Intermediate-mass black holes are among classes
Whose sizes are measured in thousands of solar masses.
The stellar-mass black holes each have a size —
Beyond three to fifteen solar masses it does not rise.
These black holes are created when individual stars collapse —
The lighter stars less than twenty solar masses perhaps.
After collapsing, neutron stars they become,
Or a white dwarf star might be the outcome.
In a micro form, a black hole might come to pass
If less than that of a star is the originating body's mass.

According to Einstein's equations' message,
A black hole is the ultimate in *spacetime warpage*,
From which it is made solely and wholly.
The phenomenon is produced by energy compacted highly
That resides within it, and not as matter.
Warpage begets warpage, nothing else whatever.
This in itself is the story whole,
And it is also the essence of a black hole.
In Einstein's equations it is remarked
Not only space near a black hole is warped,
So also time is similarly made awkward.
Nothing in time can move backward
But when the level of singularity is approaching near,
Laws of physics become less clear.
Black holes Einstein's equations predicted;
He, however, did not believe that they existed.
Research concerning black holes began to thrive,
A decade after his death, in 1955.

Quantum Gravity

My heroes during my high school years' time,
Icons of mankind are those idols of mine.
Pioneers of science mostly made my list,
Isaac Newton being my most favoured scientist.
To show my admiration I used to do one thing —
When assignments I got to improve my handwriting,
Most of the time I used to write
Some excerpt that concerned Newton's life.
One day during that period became rather unusual,
An incident occurred that was really surreal.
Written by Mahatma Gandhi, I was reading a book;
Its title was *The Story of My Experiments With Truth*.

I knew about an episode, presenting the dilemma,
Where someone had specifically asked the Mahatma
Whether there was a special reason whereby
Any occasion should prompt someone to tell a lie.
Gandhi apparently replied that if noticing somehow
That somebody was running after a cow,
To harm it, enquired at an intersection
Which way the cow had headed to seek protection,
To protect the cow in such a situation
One should point in the opposite direction.

Reading that book quite riveting,
I was on the front porch of our house sitting.
One of the walls of that front porch
Was about five feet high and it was facing north.
There was empty area just beyond that
With green grass growing, a space very flat.

Not knowing how high cows can jump
Or how it was managed, I had no hunch,
But that day a cow jumped over that wall
And landed in our porch — it did not fall!
There, my mother and myself were together alone
Sitting and relaxing, passing the afternoon.
My father and my sister were not in the house
For their personal reasons they both had gone out.
My father must have gone for his twice-daily routine
Visiting our fields — he was very keen.
My two-years-older sister perhaps had gone
To visit her friends — she left on her own.

The cow appeared to me quite bewildered
I thought it might have felt cornered.
A long cane which nearby happened to lie
I carefully picked up from close by.
I went to the porch door to open it wide
So the cow could exit outside.
The incident ended smoothly and quietly
In spite of the fact, not to be taken lightly,
That the cow had appeared agitated and delirious —
It had appeared ready to attack us.
I could have responded by hitting the cow.
I don't know whether the encounter somehow
Was affected by what I had read,
But it was a strange experience indeed.

*   *   *

From adolescence to adulthood as I grew up
My interests also changed somewhat.
When I was a medical student,
One autumn, in a youth festival event,

I happened to be selected for a mono-acting skit;
Representing my college, I was in it.
There was another performer to participate
He was my friend and classmate.
When his turn came as per the schedule
Just ahead of me, he did very well.
He was shorter than me in height.
The microphones then, to my plight,
Used to be fixed, most brands
Attached to heavy metal stands.
When my turn came to perform my skit
Perhaps from nervousness I was hit.
Up to the proper level of my own,
I forgot to adjust the microphone.
And no one else stepped in who might
Help adjust the gadget's proper height.

The crowds sitting at the back of the theatre,
Mostly a large group they were,
From a nearby women's college.
What happened to me, they had no knowledge.
So when they could not hear me speak
Spurned on by a mischievous streak
They started booing and making noise.
The chants got louder, drowning my voice.
Somehow I managed to finish my act
But at the end of it, in fact,
I felt so utterly embarrassed afterwards
And, of course, I had won no awards.
Some of my friends remained in a teasing mode
Even for a long time after the episode.
Some of the young women in the crowd
Who had booed me and were so loud
Had no bad intentions, I must say,

Later on, friendly with me were they.
The effects of the stage fright that day,
I was to realize, to my utter dismay,
Probably were going to last forever.
They killed any Bollywood dreams whatsoever,
The ones I might have hopefully nurtured
And those quietly in my mind I had pictured.

It so happened many years later
That one of my patients was a promoter.
Arrange concerts by singers and musicians he would
As well as acts by movie stars from Bollywood.
He was a gentle and likable man,
And we used to chat quite often.
Both of us discussed that if the need was there
I would provide medical care
To performers in his concerts and shows
And also the stars, howsoever they chose.
From that time whence we made the pact
Relying on me, he would often make contact
Whenever a crew member or an artist
Would fall ill, in health imperfect.
Whenever such a need was there
I provided them with medical care.
Looking back now it would appear,
In this fashion, over many a year,
I got good opportunities to meet
Several such people whom I happened to treat.

A professional in an allied medical field,
He was a casual friend and proudly once revealed
Possessing a solid background in physics
And being well-versed in many other subjects.
A big fan, he said sheepishly, with a longing for

A very glamorous female, a Bollywood star.
To our city she was to come for a show;
With a desire to meet her he was aglow.
Trying to facilitate his proposition
I promised him I would look for a solution.
I talked to the promoter, in earnest,
Revealing my friend's burning eagerness
To meet the famous female movie star —
A long-held desire he'd cherished thus far.
The promoter was quite evasive and tense,
Quite uneasy about her whims.
He told me frankly while having tea
This favour he could not guarantee,
Leaving me no chance to medically see her
Unless she developed some malady such as fever.

Not only being famous and very private,
She was unique in a manner separate,
Being a cut above all her peers,
So stunningly pretty that people would shed tears.
Even among many a famous female star,
She was the object of envy by far.
Happening to be multi-generational,
In a way, her movie-star status was special.
That gave her a real sense of confidence,
Showing comfort levels that others found defiant.
Her uninhibited aura all over the map,
That level and status her rivals could not match.
She was rebellious against many norms,
The societal decorum that prevailed in different forms.
Barely turning twenty, she was a single mother;
Her six-month-old baby did not have a father.
All this did not seem to have ill effect;
Her popularity was always at a crest.

Hundreds of millions of fans thronged
To see all the movies in which she belonged.

The unique movie star arrived as was scheduled
To give her performance to the fans who adored her.
It so happened, to her fright,
She developed a few pimples during her flight.
The promoter contacted me quickly to come over
Readily and promptly, I went to see her,
The popular movie star and the pimples on her face —
Followed were all measures I was supposed to take.
Because of the importance but non-serious nature
Treatment was done acknowledging her stature.
I also had the chance for pleasant conversation,
Sensing a strong mutual admiration.
I had felt so comfortable with her,
Hesitating somewhat, I invited her for dinner.

Being well-known as a private individual,
She was a famous star with a busy schedule.
She accepted the invitation and I was excited
Informing my friend that he was also invited.
During our chat at the dinner table
It was quite evident that she was remarkable:
A genuinely really pretty woman
And, in spite of her known curt reputation,
Very warm, intelligent and accomplished a person,
Her privacy was balanced with curiosity awesome.
Leaving her six-month-old son at home,
She had come for this concert alone.
Weaning from breast-feeding this was her first day;
She had been doing so since her son's birth day.
Obviously missing him and worried about his care
She repeatedly called home just to make sure.

My friend appeared quite mesmerized.
I let him enjoy himself, and hard he tried
To impress her somehow during the conversation,
Turning the topic towards scientific information.
The nature of the Universe with related theories, as it were,
Gave my friend the chance he needed to impress her.
Details of topics such as quantum gravity
He knew well but explained with brevity.
Mostly I remained a silent listener
While he was busy in discussion with her.

At present, one of the deepest problems arising
In theoretical physics is harmonizing
The general theory of relativity — describing gravitation
Applying to large-scale structures an explanation
Like the planets, stars and galaxies —
With quantum mechanics which we know oversees
The other three fundamental forces, namely *weak interaction*
As well as *electromagnetism* and *strong interaction*.
These act on the atomic scale, in effect.
The problem, however, needs to be put in proper context.
Contrary to a strongly held claim in particular
That the two are fundamentally incompatible —
The general theory of relativity and quantum mechanics —
It might be demonstrated, with truth in it,
That the structure of the general theory of relativity
Inevitably follows from quantum mechanics' activity.

Of theoretical massless particles interacting,
These are called *gravitons*, a name quite interesting.
In proving the existence of gravitons concretely,
Research until 2009 remained failing completely.
All quantized theories of matter necessitate
Their existence — so goes the debate.

It helps to provide this information:
Supporting this theory is the observation
That all fundamental forces, without paucity,
Have one or more messenger particles, except gravity —
Leading the researchers to believe and insist
That at least one most likely does exist.
They have dubbed these hypothetical particles
Gravitons, the name mentioned in articles.

Since the 1970s, many of the accepted notions
Unifying theories of physics that reached conclusions —
Including *string theory* or *superstring theory*,
Be it M-*theory* or *loop quantum story* —
Assume, and to some degree depend on,
Hypothesizing the existence of the graviton.
In their work, many researchers view the detection
Of the theoretical particle vital for validation.
Inconsistencies arise when scientists try
To join the quantum laws with general relativity.
Description of spacetime more elaborate,
And gravitation, relativity also gets to incorporate.
Undertaken by theoretical physicists on the whole,
Resolving these inconsistencies is a major goal.

Since it had been a long evening for her,
Expeditiously we decided to finish the dinner
So that she could get her proper rest.
On cloud nine sat my friend as he left.
For me also it had been a special evening;
I reminded her to call me if she needed anything.
No matter what time, she was not to feel guilty.
We said warm goodbyes to our famous beauty.

A few hours later she phoned and asked for me;
I had to get there fast because she needed me.
Without a chance to think or ask any question
I rushed to her place, showing no hesitation.
What I was to see when I reached her
Was really unusual and the sort of things that occur
Setting famous glamorous stars apart
From ordinary folks not in the world of art.
Being her usual voluptuous self, reclining on her bed,
She wore a very revealing gown that was coloured red.
She was in discomfort, she said, and wearing skimpy silk
Due to engorgement of her breasts caused by too much milk.
Her threshold for discomfort, being constantly pampered,
And tolerance for pain could expectedly be hampered.

What I was seeing was simply heart-stopping;
To put it mildly, absolutely jaw-dropping.
As part of her total body assets
She had large, firm and shapely tits.
Their attractiveness was already worth heeding
And was enhanced further due to breast-feeding.
For many hours, she had not breast-fed her son —
Accumulation of milk in her boobs had begun.
With tightness in her chest starting to develop,
She had phoned me but did not wait for help.
Obviously hurting from engorgement effects
She was trying to suck on her own breasts —
Stop she did not in my presence.
On the contrary, without sounding hesitant,
She made a plea that was, for me,
The height of awkwardness, as much as there could be.
In my mind, I started to realize
The reasons to acquiesce; I began to rationalize.
I was going to relieve her discomfort, I told myself,

By doing what she was doing to herself.
How many times does one with certainty
Get such an offer and opportunity? . . .
Soon after, her engorgement was gone;
The night then became very busy and long.
Compared to ones with blondes ten dozen
This experience was, by far, the best one.

In the morning hours as I was leaving
She was chirpy, with a smile teasing.
She joked that she had learned with clarity
Not only something about quantum gravity.
Winking, she said, gesturing with her hand,
"Wow! Finally, I've learned about the Big Bang!"

Instinct-Science

There was this pretty, charming young woman,
Of womanhood she was a perfect specimen.
She was very shapely and tall,
Her legs were long and her waist small.
Her narrow waist was long to the extent
That it provided an ample distance
Between her gluteus area well-developed
And her large breasts well-spread.
Each and every chiselled facial feature
All fitted to complete the perfect feminine picture.
She was twenty and her name was Sasha.
She had a friend whose name was Natasha.

In the northern English city of Middlesborough,
Sasha and Natasha were to live and grow.
Every which way, Sasha was hot;
Any which way, Natasha was not.
One more aspect, for those who cared,
Both the friends were blonde-haired.
Studying in their final school year,
Making a pact they both were to swear:
Losing their virginity in a country foreign –
Both of them were till then to remain virgin.
While Sasha remained at the virgin stage,
Natasha had gone on a rampage.
Sasha was of a nature romantic;
Natasha, on the contrary, was a nymphomaniac.
The year they both had turned twenty,
On their hands they had time aplenty –

This would be the summer they had decided on.
Visiting the province of Saskatchewan
During that summer's Canadian sojourn,
Sasha intended not to remain a virgin.

Not only covered with fields of wheat,
In many other ways is Saskatchewan unique.
One notices, standing in the green fields' midst,
The skies are blue and the air is crisp.
For miles and miles as the eye can see
Besides Nature and oneself, vastness empty.
A singing flock of birds flying in the sky
Or a herd of deer one sees, playfully passing by.
Gentle wind stroking the prairie wheat fields
A lyrically romantic symphony it yields.
If ever God Almighty had in mind
Sculpting in His image a model of mankind,
Creating the prairie people of Saskatchewan,
Is the closest in endeavour He would ever have been.
Straightforward and gentle people of this land,
The majority are of a uniformly innocent brand.
Beautiful young women bear smiles winsome,
Lots of young men are tall, blond and handsome.

Ever since arriving in the city of Regina
Natasha was focusing on filling her vagina.
In their search for suitable studs
They were regularly visiting nightclubs.
Looking one evening for a boy toy,
Drinking in a bar Natasha met a cowboy.
Sasha went back to snuggle in her bed warm
Natasha and the cowboy went to a vacant barn.

Sasha and Natasha, the next weekend at a bar,
Both spotted a hunk with a sporty car.
For the first time, Sasha's heart missed a beat —
Gushing was her heart this hunk to meet.
Inside the bar together the three went;
He told them that his name was Brent.
Intelligent and handsome, not at all coy,
Brent was a typical likable prairie boy.
He grew up on a farm as per the general rule
And he was studying in a medical school.
Sasha and Natasha had an urgent appointment —
Leaving Brent quickly, Sasha felt disappointment.

One day Brent to a get-together headed,
A group of friends for partying were gathered.
It was a typical rowdy young affair;
Sasha and Natasha also went there.
Thus a nice opportunity was produced —
Sasha to Brent was reintroduced.
Chemistry was such between Sasha and Brent,
Mutually attracted they were in an instant.
The situation somehow became complicated —
Sasha and Brent both were intoxicated.
Among the three Natasha alone remained sober;
She developed different ideas altogether.
Giving a ride to both Sasha and Brent,
Straight to the vacant barn Natasha went.
Knowing that Brent and Sasha both were drunk,
Natasha had an idea in her lustful hunt.
Leaving Sasha to sleep it off at the barn alone,
Taking Brent along, Natasha went home.

In the pre-dawn hour, Sasha became aware
She was alone — nobody else was there.

Making no sense of her surroundings at all,
Spaced out, she found it strange overall.
Things to her appeared complicated,
Though by that point she was not intoxicated.
Stepping out of the barn, there was no sound,
Just endless flatness all around.
Her wristwatch she had lost somewhere —
There was no other reference point anywhere.
At that point breathing in air rather cool
She felt as if in a surreal time capsule.
It can be said with definite certainty
Sasha that night did not lose her virginity.
Sasha was safe — leaving her on her own
And wishing her good luck, we shall move on.

*   *   *

The major components of the Universe
Constitute a variety complex and diverse.
Matter, energy, black holes and dark matter,
Including dark energy, are all the concepts that matter.
Mankind has been most tangibly familiar
With matter, since time immemorial.
Albert Einstein's famous mass-energy equation
Removed from energy the abstract notion.
For learning about the nature of the Universe,
Provoking a big leap in further progress —
The understanding of black holes and, while at it,
The attempt to understand in the process
About dark energy and also matter dark —
General relativity has provided the spark.

In all of this, *time* has remained behind the scene —
A background concept it always has been.

Keeping tabs on time mankind has been — as with matter:
The fact days and nights happen is a factor.
Seasons change with regularity, and biologic entities
Have with time their life-cycles' ties.
To all these the human psyche is connected,
So the concept of the passage of time has been developed.

Time has been a universal event-limiting factor of a kind,
Involving all the things which are known to mankind.
As a result, mankind got accustomed
To measuring various events and entities it fathomed —
In terms of time is done many a calculation.
It is measurable accurately, sans speculation.
With the progress of western civilization
There has been advanced mechanization.
Recording of things in terms of time
Became an essential step in the history of mankind.
To give some examples in this respect,
Non-western civilizations have bypassed that aspect.
To put things in perspective correct,
There have been wonderful epics, in effect,
Volumes of wisdom with a common characteristic —
Mahabharata, the Ramayana, the Vedas and such —
Where concrete chronologies were missing from the text.
Modern techniques can, to some extent, correct.
The miracles of many present-day technologies
Have been quite helpful in updating the chronologies.

At some point, with a gradual onset,
Mankind developed the mass mindset
That the flow of time follows linearity.
Einstein's equations have shown with clarity
That time can slow down, but things cannot go back in time.
Time is the fourth dimension of spacetime.

It would be interesting to step back and imagine
Not keeping tabs on time as we have come to learn.
Under a banyan tree, sitting on a cot,
Imagine a somewhat elderly man, on a spot
In the plains of northern India, without any concerns,
Not measuring time in relative terms.
His life uninterrupted by all means time-measuring,
Sense of passage of time for him should be puzzling.

All of the understanding so far developed
About the nature of the Universe has helped.
In most of the calculations in their entirety,
Time has remained an abstract, measuring entity.
Beyond a certain point near singularity
The scientists get a sense of uncertainty.
At a black hole or the Big Bang's vicinity,
There is a definite paucity of clarity.

In understanding the nature of the Universe,
I propose a new perspective for further work-up.
Coming back to the singularity problem, to wit:
It would not exist if we were to start fresh.
With the premise that makes time's identity
Three-dimensional, omnipresent, non-abstract, it is entity.
It can have a sparse and thinner stage
Or get thickened, depending on warpage,
The yet-indescribable basic units of time
With all the other components of the Universe would fit fine.
Not just exist: Time's nano-structures minute —
With all the other components, they form the loop.

About the basic time unit it is my instinct
It is Einstein's incalculable constant!
Singularities of black holes and at the Big Bang form

Concentrations of three-dimensional time in extreme form.
On some other billions-of-light-years real estate
Time just as well could be in a sparse state.
Rethinking spacetime, its space aspect
Considered would be relative and abstract.

Given a five-inch-thick clear plate of glass,
There is enough space for light to easily pass.
Passing through an elephant, the answer is negative
Because (we can argue that) space is relative.
Linear time probably is a learned concept:
For servicing human convenience this mindset does exist.
All the laws concerning Nature should be fine
And hold true in a three-dimensional time.

Instead of moving in a forward or backward line,
Things move to-and-fro in three-dimensional time.
If one walked in a pool from one spot
And then back to the same location got,
One would not encounter the same molecules of water
As one did during the first encounter.
Meaning, therefore, that one did not walk back
In the same water of the pool, was not following a track.
As far as the molecules of water are concerned
It was a to-and-fro movement as one returned.
Never mind thus travelling back in time,
One couldn't retrace, even if one kept trying,
One's path in water, molecule to molecule,
If one walked in a swimming pool.
In the given nano-time units, similarly travelling back,
Statistically it would be improbable a trap.
Given a three-dimensional, non-abstract concept of time,
Entities move to-and-fro just fine.

Constant is the speed of light, we know —
The interesting question to ask is why it is so.
The explanation could be its medium of travel;
Three-dimensional time it might unravel.
Its basic units, the photons, being in size closer
To units of time than those of matter,
Making thus bumping and blockage improbable
The speed of light is made constant and stable.

The special theory of relativity, when we contemplate
Amounts of energy, we can calculate —
Square of the speed of light it would encompass
When multiplied by the amount of a given mass.
As the theory of general relativity did predict,
Black holes have been proven to exist.
Nature of the Universe, the laws that control:
Should they hold true at a black hole?
Do black holes occupy space? I think not.
The speed of light at a black hole is reduced to naught.
At a black hole, therefore, one is to deduce,
No energy the mass-energy equation would produce.
There, at a black hole, it begs the explanation
What happens to the *mass* part of the equation?!
My hypothesis is that at a black hole
The plight of the mass of the equation on the whole
Has only one logical rhyme:
That mass there gets converted into TIME.
If only the mystery were to unravel
Why all forms of energy travel!
Could it be part of the process by which
For conversion into time they all submit?

I hope some day it will be proved
My hypothesis that eternity is cubed.